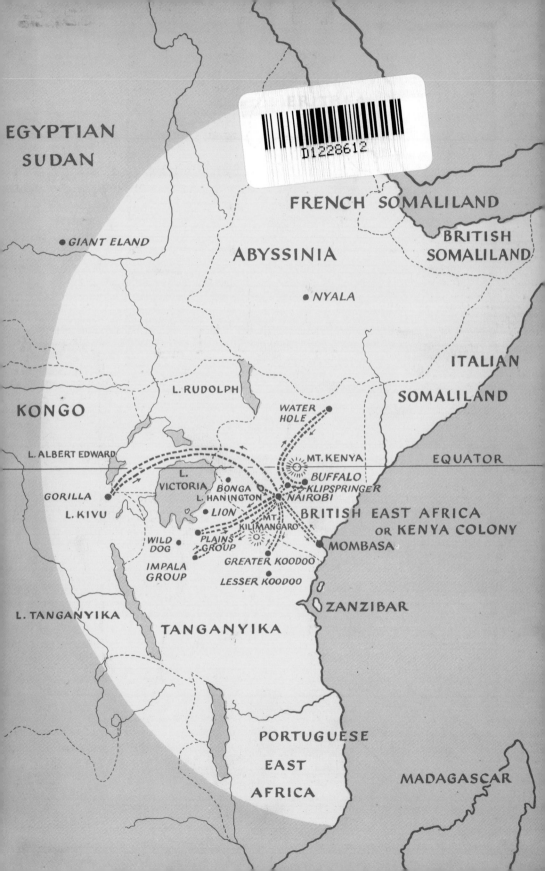

EGYPTIAN
SUDAN

FRENCH SOMALILAND

BRITISH
SOMALILAND

ABYSSINIA

• GIANT ELAND

• NYALA

ITALIAN

SOMALILAND

L. RUDOLPH

KONGO

WATER
HOLE

L. ALBERT EDWARD

EQUATOR

MT. KENYA

L.
VICTORIA

BUFFALO
KLIPSPRINGER
NAIROBI

BONGA

GORILLA

L. HANINGTON

• LION

BRITISH EAST AFRICA
OR KENYA COLONY

L. KIVU

MT.
KILIMANGARO

WILD
DOG

PLAINS
GROUP

MOMBASA

IMPALA
GROUP

GREATER KOODOO

LESSER KOODOO

ZANZIBAR

L. TANGANYIKA

TANGANYIKA

PORTUGUESE

EAST

MADAGASCAR

AFRICA

W. R. Leigh.

Nov, 23. 1938.

FRONTIERS OF ENCHANTMENT

AN ARTIST'S ADVENTURES
IN AFRICA

By W. R. Leigh

SIMON AND SCHUSTER

New York · 1938

Manufactured in the United States of America

To

Mr. and Mrs. George Lister Carlisle

Contents

vii

CONTENTS

Foreword

CARL AKELEY SELECTED ME to accompany him to
Africa in 1926 for the Museum of Natural History
of New York. He picked me because I had painted
many panoramas in Europe, and had studied twelve
years in Germany, Italy, France, and Switzerland, where
I had often been awarded prizes for pictures. He picked
me also because I had had much experience in our Western states in painting the wild life there and knew rough
camp life. He came to my studio, and after looking at
my studies said, "I'm satisfied. Take lunch with me tomorrow—we'll settle the details."

Since childhood I had devoured all the books I could
get on Africa. Sir Samuel Baker, Livingstone, Stanley,
and Colonel Patterson's *The Man-Eaters of Tsavo* were
the principal ones.

I had gathered the impression that Africa was mostly
jungle, extremely hot, pestilential, with cannibals, tsetse
flies, fever, snakes, and man-eating lions.

Most people, I find, have this idea.

But I at least knew there were no tigers in Africa.

Because the men whose works I had read had written
a long time ago did not mean to me that Africa was
greatly changed; I couldn't see how it could be.

I didn't go to the country to kill game: as a youngster

FOREWORD

I was a good hunter in Berkeley and Hampshire Counties in West Virginia where I was born. When I was five years old, I cut out of paper a thrilling scene of a man on horseback being charged by an elephant, which got first prize at the county fair at Martinsburg, West Virginia; I have the masterpiece yet. But by the time I got to Africa I was more interested in live animals than dead ones.

But when I reached the Dark Continent I found my preconception of it very faulty.

Two-thirds of Africa I found lifted between six and seven thousand feet above sea level; not hot, but gloriously delightful; a land not dark, but bright; not jungle, but open; not pestilential but extremely salubrious.

"Why," I asked myself, "have I been so mistaken in my preconceptions?"

I then realized that the men who had written so ably about Africa nevertheless did not speak my language— had not gone to look for what I did, and were not especially interested in art. Nor did they notice or dwell upon the vistas and details that, to me, were vital to the picture.

I can hear some of my scientific friends exclaiming, "Fortunately!"

Well, in spite of them I cling to my conviction, and wish some of these earlier writers had thought to conjure up such word pictures as would have permitted their readers to sense the "feel" and aroma—the glamour and romance of Africa.

If I could touch—if only lightly—some of the multiple sympathetic chords in the hearts of others; could limn what I had seen and felt with becoming skill, I was persuaded the effort would be worthwhile. Africa is an unexampled storehouse, a marvelous virgin reservoir of incomparable inspiration for painters, poets, dramatists, novelists, sculptors, and composers. It is today the world's most sublime theater for romance and adventure.

The historian and scientist need the artist to supplement their African studies—to make these more understandable, more nearly complete, more human and truthful.

Doomed all too soon to be a vanished world, Africa needs artists more than she needs the historians and the scientists.

Do I imagine myself the first and only man to sense these things? By no means. I merely feel that I am lucky enough to have come upon the scene before the novelty has been entirely worn off, and I am hopeful that my contribution may find acceptance.

FRONTIERS OF ENCHANTMENT

Chapter I

Carl Akeley

IT HAD ALL HAPPENED suddenly, unexpectedly. I had been teaching a drawing class in the New York School of Industrial Art, and one of my pupils was Arthur Jansson, who was employed at the Museum of Natural History. He had been a pupil of mine previously when I taught at the Art Students' League. One evening in 1926 Jansson asked me, "Would you consider going on a trip to Africa?"

He explained that Carl Akeley was going to Africa for the American Museum of Natural History, to secure material for groups of African animal life, which were to appear as habitat groups, mounted in their natural surroundings, in the projected new African Hall. Akeley was trying to find a painter to go with him, and make studies for the backgrounds of these groups.

Having been reared on a plantation in Berkeley County, West Virginia, I had long known our Southern forests and fauna. As a boy I had access to *Cassell's Natural History,* with its innumerable woodcuts, and had pored over its pages until I had a considerable knowledge of the wild animals of the world. I had lived and painted much in our own West. Consequently, the idea of going to Africa—that enchanted land of Livingstone, Sir Samuel Baker, and Stanley—was most attractive to me. It sounded like a glorious opportunity to a man who had always loved animals and the unspoiled phases of nature. I promptly answered, "Yes!" to Jansson's question. I had never met, or even seen, Akeley, but I arranged to do so the following day.

I met Jansson at the American Museum of Natural History the next morning, and ascending to the second floor, was introduced to Akeley. He impressed me at once as a man who had done a tremendous amount of labor, mental and physical. I judged him to be about sixty-five years old. He was neither tall nor short, slender nor heavy. He was stooped, graying, but had something dynamic and reassuring about him that made me like and trust him. I felt at once that he spoke my language. As he looked at me with his gray-blue eyes, I hoped that I made an equally good impression on him.

Akeley told me frankly that he had approached other artists. Ezra Winter, the mural painter, had come to the Museum and discussed what was wanted. He had seemed interested, but they had not arrived at an understanding. Then Willard L. Metcalf, the renowned American landscape painter, had agreed to go on the trip, but he had died. The time for departure was drawing near, and no artist of sufficient ability had been found who was willing to go. Would I show Akeley some of my work?

I invited him to my studio, where he saw many of my compositions and studies. During the years I had worked in our glamorous West I had gone in for camping and the out-of-door life. I had painted animals, landscape, clouds, and forest. In Germany I had done panoramas and murals, portraits and illustrations.

"I'm satisfied," said Akeley, after twenty minutes. "Have lunch with me tomorrow, and we'll settle the details."

We met at the appointed hour, and Akeley told me he wanted the wholehearted co-operation of the greatest artist he could get. To do the scenery for the future habitat groups would challenge the most skillful painter in the world.

We agreed that my part in the expedition would be to paint with perfect fidelity to nature; to bring to bear all the skill and knowledge I had gained during a lifetime, and thus try to make the background as convincing as the mounted animals. I was to depict the remote regions of the Belgian Congo, as wild and magically beautiful as any spot upon the globe where the gorilla dwells; to render the flowery swamplands of Kenya Colony, overlooked by the jagged peaks and glaciers of Mt. Kenya. I was to picture a rocky water hole in the semi-arid northern reaches of Kenya Colony, just south of Abyssinia, and to limn the plains of Tanganyika—those prehistoric lake beds which were once part of Victoria Nyanza.

"The backgrounds of the groups must be as correct as the animals themselves!" said Akeley. "They are as vital as the Arizona settings in your Indian and horse pictures!"

Seated on the opposite side of the table I felt with a glow of pleasure that this man was indeed the born artist of whom I had heard and read: an idealist, scientist, and poet combined. The fire radiating from Akeley lighted a flame of enthusiasm in all of us who were fortunate enough to be associated with him. It impelled us to do our best.

"I expect to be gone at least a year, perhaps longer," he said. "What are your terms?"

I named the sum for which I could give up a year; and I made it reasonable, for I longed to go.

"It's more than we have ever paid an artist," he said, "but not too much. I'll put it before the directors."

The directors agreed to my terms, and my relations with the American Museum of Natural History of New York began.

From that time until we met in Africa, two months later, I had no opportunity to become better acquainted with Akeley. He and Mrs. Akeley sailed earlier than I did; they arrived in Africa before I started. In Nairobi few chances for conversation arose. At Lukenia, for the first time, the real Akeley began to be unfolded to me. I saw him at every meal, and on many other occasions. We worked together most harmoniously.

I found that Akeley never minced words but gave things their right names. His language was sometimes unconventional, to put it mildly, but I have learned, through the years, to like men of that kind. Day by day, as we talked, I gained an insight into his lifelong battle against the small and narrow, the specious and false. I realized that I was in the company of a great—a tremendous temperament; a man who had made remarkable mechanical inventions as well as conceived and carried out artistic enterprises of profound significance. He was a great soul—a blazer of new trails.

With his artistic insight Akeley saw that all the attempts to depict Africa had failed in one essential—no

6

Carl Akeley

one had ever conveyed the savor, the feel of Africa. Many painstaking and valuable volumes had been written. There had been some painting and some sculpture. A wealth of exact data had been compiled on its animals and its native life, its minerals, geography, and flora, yet no real artist—painter or poet—had reached the true Africa, made the world sense its strange beauty, its tragic grandeur, its savage enchantment.

Akeley felt that the greatest painters, the most sublime masters of prose and verse, the mightiest of sculptors, would find in the new field of Africa a fresh inspiration; that out of the womb of that great continent would spring a virile creative art that would dwarf the outworn imagery of Europe, and make it by contrast feeble and effete.

Incidentally, he thought the book called *Black Laughter,* by Llewelyn Powys, the nearest approach that had been made toward capturing the soul of Africa.

A part of Carl Akeley's story is told in his books, but to understand the whole man, one had to know him personally. He was not talkative; one needed to study his character with sympathy, and read between the lines of his writings before the complete man was revealed.

Fifty years ago the museums of natural history everywhere made infinite contributions to our civilization. Under the direction of scientific men who had mastered their periods and fields, they appealed almost exclusively to those with the learning necessary to understand them. The average scholar did not yet feel that museums should be more democratic, more practical, and more useful to a larger proportion of the population.

The scientists of fifty years ago were conscientious, profound, and altogether admirable, but they did not envisage the educational function of museums. They did not comprehend the role that presentation—showmanship—could legitimately play in making their institutions live, exciting places. They did not perceive the morguelike coldness of their ranked exhibits or the emptiness of their halls. Yet the educational values dormant in museums were so sorely needed by the people, especially the children, that a change was inevitable.

It took a Carl Akeley to see this.

The museum authorities of those days had grown up with a deep-seated aversion to the idea of linking science and art. They could imagine nothing more incongruous or absurd than an artist in a museum of natural history! They had an abiding distrust of the painter. He was a romancer, a poet, a teller of fables in paint. He might provide a delightful source of recreation or sentimental delight, but he represented the antithesis of science. To be sure, scientists employed certain types of artist to illustrate their erudite works, but these were not regarded as artists; their products were craftsmanship, not true art. With craftsmen they could work harmoniously, but the other kind had ideas of their own; therefore they were anathema in a scientific institution.

In this atmosphere of disapproval a bombshell exploded in 1895. The man who threw it was a brilliant young artist who hailed from a farm.

Akeley once told me the whole story. He had taken a job with a commercial taxidermist in Rochester. At first the work seemed wonderful, but in a short time he became conscious of sordid commercialism, fakery, slipshod methods, an utter absence of ideals. He had grown up among animals and birds, and their marvelous beauty, the matchless ingenuity and subtlety of nature's handiwork, had stamped itself indelibly upon his consciousness. He knew that his boss was turning out incorrect, inartistic, vulgar, contemptible work.

He could not continue in such an atmosphere; it stifled, nauseated him. Yet taxidermy itself interested and attracted him; it had tremendous possibilities! Whereupon he drifted into the Milwaukee Museum, only to find himself almost as much dissatisfied as in the first place.

Until Akeley rebelled, animals had been stuffed with hay, excelsior, rags, anything. The unscientifically tanned pelts covered unstable, makeshift frames. Imperfectly cured hides on shaky underpinnings could not endure. We have all seen, hanging on proud walls, sorry heads of elk or moose. Their antlers, which should have been boldly erect, drooped dejectedly or tilted to one side. What made them so unnatural and ridiculous? The stuffing had given way under the strain of shrinking hide and the weight of horns.

Akeley soon realized that the art of taxidermy must be revolutionized. He felt that fate had assigned him to this task, and he applied his gigantic energy, his rare inventive talent, and his artistic genius to master the problems involved.

He had never learned much about art in any school. When he began he knew almost nothing, technically speaking, of drawing, painting, sculpture, or taxidermy:

his education had been simple in the extreme, yet the artistic impulse burgeoned insistently within him. He knew: nobody had to tell him. He saw, as clearly as in blazing sunlight, things that none of his contemporaries saw. Luckily for the world, he was endowed with unyielding tenacity of purpose, and could not be discouraged or dissuaded, for he saw what he saw too clearly to be affected by the less clear-sighted.

He evolved a new technique in mounting animals.

Rumors of his accomplishments spread. The Field Museum in Chicago summoned him. It was from there that this extraordinary man first compelled the notice of a preoccupied world.

But he continued to meet with cynical skepticism and hostility. In the Field Museum animals were also still being stuffed. Akeley's descriptions of what ought to be —of what he could create—startled and baffled the museum authorities. Yet all of them put together could not equal the brilliant imagination, the dynamic energy, the determination of the newcomer. He was not afraid to stand alone; he was not timid; he never shrank from battle. With the purest logic and soundest taste he routed his opponents. Sullenly, grudgingly, slowly, opposition diminished. The directors, the financial lords of the community, the press, the intelligence of the nation, began to be stirred.

Finally the Field Museum purchased Akeley's *Four Seasons*—habitat groups representing deer during summer, autumn, winter, and spring. These put Akeley in a class by himself. Not only did his new taxidermy doom stuffing and usher in the mounting of animals; it presaged unmistakably the era of the painter in museums.

11

The possibilities of the habitat group began to dawn upon the minds of men.

In 1909 Carl Akeley joined the staff of the American Museum of Natural History of New York City, and thereafter gave it seventeen years of his life.

When he first described to its incredulous directors his vision of the African Hall, they shuddered and gasped at the staggering cost, the stupendous labor.

Years had to elapse, and a whole hall of small bird groups had to be completed, before the Museum authorities were ready to consider the African Hall project. And Akeley himself had to find the funds with which to make a start.

The 1926 expedition which I accompanied was Akeley's fifth trip to Africa. He wrote: "Soon I shall be on my way to Africa; this time accompanied by artists and taxidermists, happy that my years of preparation are ended and my big work actually begun!"

Chapter II

Lukenia

M Y FIRST REALIZATION of the glories of Africa came to me when we arrived at the Lukenia Hills, in Kenya Colony, twenty miles away from civilized Nairobi, in the midst of the marvelous plains named for the winding Athi River.

The sun was just rising as I stepped out of my tent. I had established myself close to the upstanding central wall of the pink granite ridge—a miniature mountain range running north and south. The comb of rock above us shut off the sun's shafts at that early hour, but they flooded a rocky hill to the westward in a magical rose-amber light. A wisp of lazy smoke ascended in a lustrous pink-lilac line from a Wakamba hut on this hillside, while the dried grass of which the hut was built glowed orange-red.

The rocks cast long shadows that undulated in streaks of lavender across the rolling terrain we had climbed from the plains. Occasional granite *kopjes* in the range of hills caught the scintillating pink light of the morning on their naked crests, while their shadowed sides remained cool violet and mauve.

I filled my lungs with the pure, sweet air, and felt as if I were drinking wine. I flung out my arms as if to embrace the intangible genius of the place—of this sun-bathed, enchanting Africa!

13

Sunrise over Lukenia

LUKENIA

Nobody else was astir in camp except the cook and his two helpers, who were preparing breakfast.

As I gazed to the south at a large *kopje* which towered against the sky a scant half-mile away, I became aware of a puzzling activity on its summit. Peering through my field glasses, I found myself looking at baboons in their natural surroundings for the first time in my life. Yes, baboons—a gang of them, big and little, all squatting, and trying to make out what *I* was. Presently I beheld an old-man baboon, apparently peeved, start toward a youngster; the latter, wise through experience, leaped from the top of the rock and landed on a tree below. I made up my mind that as soon as breakfast was over I would explore that *kopje*.

For the moment I simply climbed the backbone of the ridge near camp. When I reached the top I discovered that the easterly side fell precipitately several hundred feet to vast rolling plains, streaked with watercourses and flecked with flat-topped acacia trees. Receding, wave upon wave, fading into pearl and lavender shadows, the plains ended in another elevation, infinitely delicate in its hazy loveliness, over whose long, smooth sweeping lines cascaded the splendor of the sun. Sparkling, coruscating, twinkling, the effulgent light invested every object with a grace and glory that belong only to this hour. Cobwebs on grass and bush shimmered, lacy trees were touched with glints of gold, anthills and small *kopjes* were splashed with amber and saffron.

In its glow and glitter and silvery immensity the land seemed tenantless—uninhabited. But as I continued to look I discovered moving dots: the plains were alive with herds of animals! Tiny as they were in the distance,

15

I identified impala in the nearest group and odd-shaped hartebeest not far removed; I made out zebra and many gazelle. The scattering herds stretched away over the crests of gentle hills, across flat plains, blending with groves of trees, until they finally merged into the lilac haze.

I was enchanted. For the first time I beheld primitive Africa—the unspoiled, glorious Africa of which I had dreamed.

At breakfast we all assembled around our table in the dining tent, which was open at each end, and roomy enough for the waiters to pass behind us on either side.

The party included Mr. and Mrs. Akeley, A. A. Jansson, R. C. Raddatz, and myself. We expected R. H. Rockwell to join us here. George Eastman, Daniel Pomeroy, and Dr. Stewart, Eastman's physician, were to meet us later.

Breakfast over, I set off to explore the massive pile of granite where I had seen the baboons. As I neared it I happened to glance at a boulder which stood up above the surrounding bush near the base of the *kopje*. Suddenly on the summit of the boulder a little antelope appeared. It had not been there a moment before, but had evidently leaped up from behind the rock to get a better look at me. Instantly I knew that I was looking at a klipspringer. It was a diminutive antelope, no bigger than a fox terrier, but not so heavy, and it had sharp two-inch black horns. My natural history studies had made me familiar with the creature's appearance, but this was the first live one I had ever seen. We regarded one another some moments, but when I tried a shot with my kodak, the little buck vanished.

LUKENIA

I had hoped the baboons would still be on the *kopje*, but when I reached it none were to be seen. The granite mass on which I had seen them playing consisted of two enormous boulders wedged together between pronglike masses of upstanding rock. Immediately back of these were other huge and more solidly attached formations, separated by a great rift. Under and between the twin boulder masses some cavernous holes spurred my curiosity. I approached them through bushes and cactus plants, long grass and tangled creepers, and over the tumbled fragments of fallen rock. Squirming in and out, I climbed steadily upward, carefully avoiding the cracks and fissures, which apparently sank into the bowels of the earth. I made for the largest cavity, an eerie and forbidding aperture, about which hung a disturbing odor. There was a slick, worn, and yellowish look about the rocks at the opening—beasts of prey must have rubbed against them when gliding in and out of their dens.

"What sort of reek is that?" I asked myself, sniffing the air. Cats!

Yes, surely, cats—but leopards or lions, which? I listened intently, peering into the dusky recesses. As my sun-dazzled eyes became accustomed to the obscuring gloom, dim whitish objects began to reveal themselves. They were bones—all of herbivores—antelope, big and little. But—yes, there was a sheep skull with one horn still attached. I reached down into a rock pocket and picked up a hair—a tawny hair—from what kind of beast? A goat, a kongoni, possibly a lion. Had the wind wafted it here or had it fallen from a victim that was being carried in?

17

Baboons in the Lukenia Hills

LUKENIA

My imagination promptly produced a picture: midnight; goats and sheep drowsing in the Wakamba thorn corral which I had so lately seen on the sunlit hillside. I fancied that scene in moonlight, the stillness interrupted only by a restless lamb snuggling closer to its mother, or just inside the inclosure the herder muttering in his sleep. A flashing form—a thud—pandemonium! How easy it was to reconstruct a tragedy from bleached bones and a tawny hair! Did the nocturnal marauder still linger here?

I sniffed, looked, listened.

A cricket squeaked faintly somewhere deep in the rocks—a grasshopper chirruped not far away.

After all, the pungent cat odor was stale; there was no hint of dried blood or decaying meat; there were no green flies about. No, the place was untenanted. Reassured, I climbed into the cleft, and found that the far end opened on a sunlit cliff beyond. Toward this I made my way through the cool, deep shade between two mighty masses of rock, roofed by a third, high above my head. A little light sifted through the crack between them, and the sunlit cliff reflected a glimmer. Finally I reached the opposite side where I stood on smooth slabs of stone which were separated from the cliff by a chasm fully fifty feet deep, but only some eight feet across.

I wished some master geologist might explain to me by what convulsions, or slow mutations, nature had achieved these strange and dramatic results. What giant forces had tumbled together these Gargantuan pebbles among which I crept like a midge?

I made my way back through the cave to my starting point, and, once more on open ground, proceeded around

19

the edge of the *kopje,* seeking a favorable point from which to ascend.

As I stood looking over the lesser boulders strewn up the side, a gray lizard some six inches long caught my eye. It was crouching, flat on its belly, something in the manner of a panther; I had never seen a lizard do just this before. Looking for the explanation, I observed a grasshopper basking on the same flat sunlit rock, three feet away. Some fragments of stone lay between them, and a little grass was growing from a crack in the rock. I realized that the lizard was stalking the grasshopper. With consummate cunning and skill the little killer crept nearer, while the unsuspecting prey chirruped merrily, blithely waving its antennae, oblivious of danger. The lizard paused, gathered himself, and then propelled his body like a tiny rocket, landing on top of the grasshopper. The two rolled over and over in desperate battle, but with teeth and talons the ferocious little saurian soon put the fate of his victim beyond doubt.

Here, in miniature, I saw enacted one of those terrific scenes of the dim Cretaceous period, when the monstrous Tyrannosaurus, leaping into the air, descended upon the defenseless duck-billed Trachodon. Here, reduced in size merely, Tyrannosaurus still survived, as efficient as ever, in a tiny world all his own. He was the king of killers then. Today, smaller, somewhat less ethical, he remains the more or less direct descendant of the supreme killer. The world has not changed so much, after all!

Picking my way up through bushes and over boulders to the summit of the *kopje,* I found myself standing on the flat top of a slab of gray-pink granite, looking over a sharp edge into a large pit with a sloping granite floor,

some forty feet below. On all sides of this irregular pit
rose perpendicular walls of the same height as the one
over which I stood. It was easy to see that they had once
all been one, but during the eons cracks had formed, and
those on the sloping side of the domed underlying rocks
had slipped, while mine, on the crest of the dome, had
stood still. On the opposite side from which I had ascended I looked down upon several hundred feet of
chaotically jumbled bush tangles and upstanding rocks.

Many times in America, alone in wild places, I used
to sit perfectly still, and watch for things to happen.
When a man moves about in such regions, many eyes, of
which he is unconscious, observe him, but if he remains
immovable for twenty minutes, the owners of these eyes
are reassured, and begin to move about themselves. If
you do not move, you become to these creatures just another rock or tree stump. I have had mice and squirrels
climb up on my lap to obtain food; birds have lit on my
head; rabbits have played all around me; I have had
wild turkeys look at me long and carefully, and then go
on with their accustomed search for acorns and chest-
nuts.

So it was in Africa. In full view, silhouetted against
the sky, I sat on the top of the *kopje* and waited, and by
the time five minutes had elapsed things began to happen. On the floor of the pit, below me, under the edge of
one great rock slab, a depression in the rocky floor left
an eight-inch opening between floor and slab. Here I
spied eight little feet, the animals they belonged to being
hidden from me on my high perch by the overhanging
rock. They were curious little feet, with clawless toes.

Presently the owners—two queer little tailless fellows

about the weight of a woodchuck, and of a brindle-brown color—came out from under the rock into the sunlight. I had never seen or even read of such creatures. Later Akeley told me that the animals were hyraxes, whose nearest relative is the hippopotamus, and that the suction of their spongy, rubberlike feet enables them to climb rocks and trees amazingly.

I turned my head to look down over the eastern side of the *kopje,* and was soon rewarded by seeing a klip-

Hyrax

springer bound to the top of a rock, and look at me with surprise and curiosity. Soon his mate joined the inspection, while a third browsed on the ground, concluding, no doubt, that I was deadly uninteresting. Shifting my body gradually to look behind me, I beheld not far away, on the level ground, a three-foot-tall secretary bird. His long legs, his head and beak like a hawk's, the quills of his feathered crest lying obliquely back on his neck, and his long tail made a queer combination. I knew about

Secretary birds

him from my natural history—a freak, but a handsome one.

Now, what was that bird doing? He was stalking around one spot in a perfectly ridiculous fashion, constantly watching the center of the circle he was making. Because of the high grass I could not see what he saw, but presently he paused, faced the center of the ring, and slowly raised one of his long, awkward turkey feet until it almost touched his breast. Then, like lightning, it shot out and down. My mounting suspicion was confirmed when the crested head dropped into the grass and rose again holding by the tail an eighteen-inch snake, limp and unresisting. The reptile had been knocked out by the blow from the bird's foot. The stately snake slayer calmly swallowed the tidbit, and stalked away in quest of more. I discovered later that a pair of these grave birds, which nest in trees, lived not far from our camp, but we could never discover just where, although we saw them often. They flew with their long legs straight out behind, like cranes, and volplaned skillfully. Their unbeautiful song sounded like hollow bones clapped together, but it was agreeably short.

What with the secretary bird, whose food is serpents, and the mongoose, who devours both the reptiles and their eggs, Africa has a sparse snake population, less, in fact, than most other parts of the world. Those snakes one does encounter are usually large, having somehow eluded their enemies until they became too formidable for easy capture.

The mongoose is said to vanquish serpents as much as eight feet long, but some specimens, notably the rock python, which grows to a length of twenty feet, or more, are too much even for the mongoose. Two natives arrived one day at this Lukenia camp of ours to report that a *nyoka mcubwa* (big snake) had swallowed their dog! It hardly seemed possible. We went after the dog eater, which proved to be a python over fourteen feet long, and we soon had his handsome hide drying over the rear end of our truck. But the guzzled dog was beyond aid. Akeley said this one was "not a big snake."

Besides the python, there are cobras as much as twelve feet long, black, brown, and green mambas that reach a length of six to ten feet, and adders of five or six feet. All of these reptiles, except the python, are poisonous, yet the mongoose will tackle them with marvelous courage and adroitness, and after a hair-raising battle, kill them. It ought to be against the law for anybody to harm a mongoose.

After watching the secretary bird, I moved on to the point where lately I had seen the baboons, and found the top of the rock foul with their droppings. From here I could see the people moving about in our camp, and realized readily how we must have puzzled the simians.

As I stood on the rock I had a magnificent view of the Athi plains, formerly one of the most famous hunting grounds in the world. Fifteen years before, it was crowded with incalculable hundreds of thousands of animals. I recalled that Akeley had once described to me the vast herds of grazing beasts he had seen on his first visit here. Looking about me, I realized that now comparatively few were left. Herbivores eat grass, lions eat herbivores; when the grass eaters leave a region the meat-eaters must follow. Perhaps the deserted den I had

The Athi plains and Lukenia Hills

passed through needed no other explanation. Although
I couldn't see them, I knew that game trails, sometimes
several inches deep, crisscrossed the whole plain below
me. The trails of the herbivorous beasts wound sinuously
along in the open grass, avoiding the rocks and gullies,
while the carnivores' tracks crept in and out among the
rocks, hugging the backbone ridges.

Some twenty miles distant, a little to the right of the
last hill in our range, rose the blunt rounded bulk of
Kilima-mbogo (Buffalo Mountain), and to the left,
many miles beyond, the delicate blue silhouette of Mt.
Kenya appeared soon after sunrise, looming over 17,000
feet, and wreathed in clouds. Despite the distance I could
see its glaciers—glaciers which fill a crater lake, where
all the year round the people of Nairobi may go skating,
in spite of the fact that the equator runs directly across
the mountain!

This, the second highest elevation in Africa, can be
scaled as far as the lake by automobile, but its peaks
have never been ascended and are sometimes invisible
for months at a time in clouds.

Looking southward I beheld the snow-covered dome
of Kilimanjaro, 19,328 feet, the highest mountain in
Africa. It lay two hundred miles away, on the northern
border of Tanganyika. About all I could see of it was
the shimmering cream-rose fields of its snowy crest; its
shadow side looked so much like the surrounding sky
that at first glance the sunlit snow seemed a glistening
apparition. This exquisitely delicate Mountain of Demons refused to remain part of our prosaic earth; it was
a glimpse of fairyland suspended in space!

Just as I was about to leave the *kopje* I caught sight

of my baboon clan returning over the crest of the rocks. They had not seen me, so I crouched behind a boulder and waited for them as they advanced slowly, methodically turning over stones in search of crickets and beetles and ants' eggs. Their movements were comically suggestive of deliberate, jerky little old dwarfish men. The youngsters were pert and frisky, the older ones sedate and businesslike. The males had great bushy manes, long horse faces, and alert hazel eyes set close together. The females carried babies on their backs.

As they approached me one of the smart-aleck youngsters, in advance of the rest, caught sight of the upper part of my grinning face peeping over the rock. Not more than thirty feet away he paused abruptly and fixed me with an accusing stare; I winked at him. This amazed and outraged his sensibilities, but he was so fascinated that he could not take his eyes off me. I raised my head sufficiently to display my countenance twisted into a grimace. He got almost beside himself with wrath, but curiosity still held him. I screwed my face into a series of contortions, and stuck out my tongue at him. Then he could stand it no longer. He began to bounce up and down on his rock, and to denounce me violently: "Oho! Oho! Oho!" This brought all the rest in a rush to see what was the matter. One old-man baboon, when he reached the side of the youngster, paused, lowered his head between his shoulders, thrust it forward, and fixed me with a German medical-student stare. When I suddenly jerked my hand up and thumbed my nose at him, he showed his teeth, and jerked himself to his full height, with all his mane bristling. A younger, more incautious male again began an exasperated bark: "Oho! Oho! Oho!"

LUKENIA

I suddenly let out a bloodcurdling Comanche yell which flung the baboon family into a panic; they collided—ran over each other. One little chap keeled over on his back, rolled off the rock he was on, and, thinking himself in imminent peril, came up fighting. Finding there was nothing to fight, he bounded away. But the old man did not retreat far. He turned with his mouth open and his long yellow fangs bared. His hazel eyes had turned fiery red. I screwed my face into fiendish contortions. Finally he made up his mind not to be bluffed. He took two stiff-legged jumps toward me and emitted an infuriated "Oho! Oho! Oho!" Then a tempest of ohoing from the more courageous of the tribe, which had halted at some distance, rent the air with all the maledictions and epithets of the baboon language!

I sprang to my feet with a roar, and the whole band, in a mad scramble, scurried over the rocks helter-skelter, wildly indignant, but no longer in doubt that caution was the better part of valor.

On my way back to camp I noticed a huge roundish boulder that rose some forty feet into the air, isolated on a floor of granite. It was bare of vegetation, and as I circled it I saw no possibility of climbing up any side. More than all the other rocks it tantalized the imagination. By what freakish chance had it come to rest there? Could any animal scale it? That question was answered in a short time.

My first morning in the real Africa—uncivilized Africa—had started well. Full of enthusiasm, I returned to camp, where I began preparations to paint my studies for the klipspringer group.

Akeley and I went together to the same big *kopje*

and, after we had climbed about halfway up at almost the same point I had ascended before, we faced north.

"Here," said Akeley, "is the place I picked out when I was last here; I want a portrait of this view!"

It was superb. On my right rose the great wall of rock, and beside it the tree to which the little baboon had leaped. The foreground was composed of bushes and rocks extravagantly colored by lichens. Beyond these we looked down upon the backbone of our ridge, receding sinuously. Our tents among the scattered acacias looked like children's toys. Beyond them the ridge ended in a high rocky mass which lay under a cloud shadow—a purple eminence against a vast expanse of sunlit plain— a fabric woven of gold and silver. Kilima-mbogo was somewhat to the right, and on the left, about four miles away, the Athi River pursued its serpentine course into the opalescent distance. Finally, majestic Mt. Kenya lifted its glacial peaks that looked like pale shadows above its belt of clouds. I was delighted to have the opportunity to paint that splendid scene.

We decided on the forenoon as the best time of day, and I set to work at once. Akeley had a fly set up on the site, and started at once to build the field model for the klipspringer group, with the scene I was painting as background. We also used the fly as a retreat during showers, which were still frequent, and we stowed my studies and paraphernalia under it at night.

Akeley was in buoyant spirits that morning: he was back once more amid the scenes of his first trip to Africa in 1896.

Chapter III

The Klipspringer

K LIPSPRINGER IS A DUTCH or Boer word. It means cliff jumper, and refers to the creature's unrivaled ability to climb cliffs and leap chasms. The animal stands some twenty-two inches high, and is found throughout Africa south of the Sahara. It lives exclusively among rocks and, of all hoofed animals extant, performs the most incredible feats of climbing.

The klipspringer group was planned to show as its central feature the klipspringer and, secondarily, the baboon; the hyrax was to play a part also, as was the honey bird. This last is about the size of a sparrow, and of a steel-blue color. It is not a hummingbird, yet subsists upon honey.

The natives of Africa believe that this bird will try to lead or decoy a man to a bees' nest, with the hope of feasting upon what he leaves after rifling the hive, or perhaps upon the grubs, when the hive is opened. I saw many honey birds, but never attempted to follow one.

Because the klipspringer's archenemy is the leopard, the tiny antelope must spend his nights upon the tops of inaccessible rocks. There are not many such rocks, and as baboons are forced by the same enemy to observe similar precautions, the safe rocks, by some unknown method of mutual agreement, are divided by the two animals. Certain rocks are monopolized by klipspringers;

31

Leopard on the prowl

others by baboons. During the day the mother klip-springers leave their babies on these rocks while they descend for food and drink. How the babies get to the tops of the rocks is an unsolved mystery. It is my belief that they are born there, and never descend until old and strong enough to climb back.

It may be assumed that the klipspringer is also preyed upon by eagles and rock pythons, but I had no opportunity to observe this. What defense it could have against these two enemies I do not know. On the exposed tops of their rocks the kids do not move about, but lie still, so that, although exposed to view from above, their coloration blends with the pink granite, on which they look like so many lichen blotches. Quite probably pythons could not climb to the tops of the rocks where the kids lie, but as certain high rocks of this range were the habitual perches of birds of prey, I wondered how the kids escaped.

Besides, wild dogs, jackals, and hyenas were all enemies; I often wondered how there could be any klip-springers left.

Since the klipspringer never strays from his rocks, and these are rarely in the neighborhood of streams or lakes, it would seem that his only source of water must be the juices of the vegetation he consumes. During the rainy season, of course, there are water pockets galore in the rocks, but none during the long dry season.

The klipspringer has a highly specialized hoof, unlike that of any other herbivore. These hoofs are small, pointed downward, and have sharp edges, so they can catch on the slightest unevenness. The animal is almost wholly silent. The only sound I ever heard a klipspringer

33

Klipspringer at Lukenia

make was the cry of warning given by one on the lookout. This consisted of a brief, sharp note, not very loud, and sounded once only. From its large bright eyes and oversize ears, forever sensitively moving, catching the slightest sound, and its small nostrils, it seems clear that the creature depends for safety on hearing and sight, not scent.

We had an illustration of the uncanny climbing ability of the klipspringer shortly after our arrival at Lukenia. Akeley went out to get a few specimens of the animal, and when he neared the huge isolated boulder I have described, he saw a klipspringer standing on its summit. When he fired, the animal leaped into the air and fell dead an amazing distance from the rock. Akeley and I afterward tried to figure out how the little antelope, having nothing but his hoofs to climb with, could possibly have made the forty-foot ascent. Neither of us could see how anything short of claws could cling to the rock even at the most favorable point. The boulder was sharply undercut except at one place, where the overhang ended not more than six feet up—a possible leap. But from that point the rock was practically perpendicular for more than ten feet before it began to slope, very gradually, toward the top. On this perpendicular surface there were places where slivers of rock had scaled off, but the edges left were not more than a quarter of an inch at their widest points, and these points were irregular and scattered, with wide gaps between them. The animal might have leaped the six feet of overhang, but how he clung and kept his balance thereafter was inconceivable. Nothing seemed more obvious than that he could not have done what he did.

Later on, while I was painting studies among the rocks, two of these creatures came near, and because I kept very still they stood quietly within twenty feet of me. I almost was afraid to breathe lest I alarm them. I was evidently an object of engrossing interest, with my umbrella, palette, and big canvas; they studied me and I studied them. They stood beside an overhanging rock some twenty or thirty feet high. Wind and rain had hollowed it out below, and left a narrow bench five feet above where they stood. With apparently no preparation or effort one of the animals bounded up and landed there, where he remained standing, though the floor of the bench sloped so steeply that I marveled at his effortless composure.

We arrived at Lukenia toward the end of the wet season. From our high hill we could see the sun rise and set each day, and we often stood speechless before the marvelous pageantry of clouds. Each afternoon highpiled heaps of cumulus clouds filled the cerulean sky, rolling and crowding each other, casting their shadows in purple and lavender across the vast topaz and old-rose plain. Often these cloud masses shimmered in ineffable splendor above, while beneath they were pouring a flood of rain. Sometimes we could see six or seven showers at one time. I never saw a rough, wild storm in Africa.

There were two kinds of weather disturbances. At Lukenia, almost every day there were sudden showers lasting perhaps only a few minutes, and stopping as quickly as they started. Sometimes, however, we would wake in the morning under a leaden sky tinged with an ominous green, and from this canopy abruptly descended a perpendicular flood of rain. Beginning so, the rain might last all day and into the night. No work was possible, and we were driven to take refuge in our tents.

On such an evening I found it very pleasant to lie snug in bed, covered with the crazy quilt and Navaho blankets I had brought from home, with my bedside candle-lantern lit and a book to read, while the rain gustily pelted the sides of my tent, and all outdoors was as black as the nether pit—a blackness undreamed of by city dwellers.

There was neither thunder nor lightning with such storms—just a quiet downpour. I heard the rain trickling from the tent fly into my collapsible bathtub, which Peater, my tent boy, had promptly placed in an advantageous position to catch water. It was getting fuller and fuller. I heard the water gurgling gently in the ditch Peater had dug around the tent. Every sound was soothing. It was difficult not to be lulled to sleep, although it was early. That steady patter-patter was so pleasant.

I could hear the little streamlets from the ditch and the overflowing bathtub join forces and go joyfully on down the hill, where they fell in with other jolly little streamlets, until together they began to sound self-conscious, cocky, and arrogant, and rattle and splash among the stones. At the bottom of the hill, they joined the brawling, intrepid creek that roars and boils among the boulders and ledges, contemptuous of all obstacles, jostling its raging way peremptorily, until its turbulent passion is calmed on the broad bosom of the Athi River, whose quiet is not disturbed by such trivialities as showers.

I had glimpsed my first rhinos here at Lukenia, and

I could fancy them, with the slow-moving hippos and crocodiles, basking in the rain as they do in the sunlight, and satisfied that it was a glorious wet night. Even the frogs sang its glory.

The seductive patter kept up a gentle tattoo; the candle grew short; my eyes would not stay open; the rain won. When I opened them again the patter had ceased, the stars were out, and I could see the distant lights of Nairobi from my tent door.

Most of the time there was clear, sparkling sunshine, never oppressively hot. Under these conditions, to paint the plains with absolute fidelity was no fool's job. It required straight-from-the-shoulder, honest-to-God painting, and no nonsense. The fellow who tackled it had to know his stuff.

I never enjoyed working more in my life; I was painting the most enchanting subjects under conditions de luxe. Previously, when painting in Arizona, New Mexico, South Dakota, Wyoming, or other places, I had had to shift for myself—lug my paintbox, umbrella, canvas, and campstool myself, no matter what the distance, and it was often miles.

But in Africa I was a king! I had a gun boy, who carried all my luggage, while I carried the gun. I soon trained my boy to help me get everything in readiness for work. When distances were to be covered I took a closed truck, and in this the wet study, tied in a suitable position and covered with a wagon sheet, was protected from dust and rain. In the field the boy took the gun, and sat down back of me to keep guard, for in a land like Africa there is never any telling when, while you are engrossed, some creature may start stalking you from behind. When we reached camp in the evening my gun boy washed the brushes very efficiently. It was ideal, and incidentally enabled me to complete many more studies than I could have done without such help.

My first gun boy was an Abyssinian, Ibrahim, as black as tar, and very intelligent. He gloried inordinately in handling a fine rifle; it was to him a thing of beauty and a visible evidence of superiority, like a string of medals across the chest of a hero.

The British do not allow the blacks to own rifles, but every native aspires to the privilege of handling one. Ibrahim knew how to care for a gun, as he had been an *asikari* (soldier) in Nairobi. He wore a red fez, khaki coat and breeches, and wrapped puttees—but no shoes! For hours he would sit watching me paint, while he kept careful watch on all sides for enemies. In the evenings around the campfire, as he and his friends cooked their chunks of meat, he discoursed learnedly on how the *"bwana akafanya sanamu"* (master paints pictures). Later on he would tell Arabian Nights' tales, richly embroidered, I gathered.

To me it was a sheer luxury—matchless privilege— to have nothing to do but paint under these ideal conditions, in ideal weather, in an ideal country—just paint— paint—paint!

Under such conditions, perched on the side of the big *kopje,* from the spot Akeley and I had together selected, I painted my comprehensive study of the view for the klipspringer group. Akeley was delighted, as the study developed. The dream of his life was coming true, he said. During all his previous trips he had regretted that he was not a painter, able to preserve these scenes, and now it was being done—done in the way he had wished he could do it.

In our talks, Akeley said, "We must set a standard to which others will have to rise," and, "Only masters can adequately handle the problems involved." He also said, "The landscape painter who has cultivated a style or manner is not any good . . . the painted background must display a complete unity with the mounted animals. The painter must make the beholder forget that he is looking at paint, and feel that he is looking at nature itself. A very high type of artistic knowledge is necessary for this. . . . The artist must forget himself in his work."

After I had finished the large study, at Akeley's request I painted a second view of the plains to be presented to the Governor of Kenya Colony and hung in Government House at Nairobi.

Besides these, I executed a number of smaller studies, all of which I judged would help in the carrying out of the group in the proposed African Hall.

One afternoon Akeley called me into his tent, where Mrs. Akeley sat with him. When I had taken a seat Akeley came straight to the point, as was his wont.

"I don't believe anybody is better fitted to do the groups in African Hall than you are," he said. "We've been talking it over. How would you like to take charge of the painting, be the art director of the African Hall?"

I had been wondering who would be entrusted with this important post. I answered him with equal frankness: "I know that you and I together could make it the finest thing of its kind in the world."

40

Chapter IV

New Things

THE CHARM OF LUKENIA. . . . How good it was just to be alive there! Good just to sit and watch the grasses wave, the butterflies bobbing about over the flowers. Good to lie on one's back and gaze up into the limpid blue of the zenith, to listen to the cry of the horn-bills overhead, and the chirping of the hyraxes in the rocks. It was deeply interesting to note every leaf and every blade of grass, every shrub and tree—all so different from the flora of America. And the ants, the grass-hoppers, the moths, the flies were all different.

Queer twisted trees, like none I had ever seen, bore brilliant, exotic, bee-attracting blossoms! The table-topped acacias were puzzling; what had produced that flat top? The wild fig, too, amazed me.

The fig is one of the strangest of trees. It starts out in life as a delicate little creeping vine, seeking something to climb upon. As soon as it finds a host-tree it begins to climb and grow with extraordinary and ferocious exuberance, unique, I believe, in the vegetable kingdom. The wild fig accommodates itself to all conditions and circumstances; it swiftly monopolizes its host-tree, encircling it with coil upon coil of cables, that grip with a relentless, strangling hold. The pathetic victim of its savagery droops and slowly expires; with spasmodic effort it puts out a branch, only to have it promptly en-

41

circled; it bends and twists like an animal trying to extricate itself from the rings of the pythonlike embrace. All struggle is futile. The host dies, but not before the fig has itself become a tree, built up of monstrous bands that gradually straighten, binding themselves into a huge trunk, with a gaping well in its center—the hole left by the original host, rotted and turned to dust. With a wild, rampant energy the fig puts out long branches: it drops hundreds of slender suckers from its limbs that creep down fifteen, twenty feet, until they reach the ground and take root. It flattens itself out over rocks in broad shields, and splits the rocks by gliding into crevices. It grows to huge proportions, and with its dense shade smothers out all undergrowths. It is a veritable octopus of the vegetable world. The feeble thing that groped its precarious way along the ground, pitifully, humbly, seeking aid, has become a giant, a merciless usurper, an insatiable vampire.

I saw some wild fig trees with trunks six feet in diameter, and sending out vast arms. I once mounted the descending branch of one of these leviathans a hundred feet from the stem, and walked as on a roadway up to the trunk itself, where I found myself over thirty feet above the ground.

Under the bark of other trees I discovered termites silently, invisibly at work. One sees a fine large tree growing yellow and sere for no apparent reason. It sickens like human beings we have seen, stricken by some physical blight, slowly succumbing to a secret, creeping death. Presently the great tree is dead; only its stark form remains erect. Then, some day, without warning, the giant telescopes—collapses. The shell of bark can support it no longer, and it slumps in ruins, its interior reduced to dust. For years the insidious insects have undermined, sapped the life currents of the tree. Thus whole forests are wiped out of existence by a creature so small, so delicate that it cannot endure the light of day, and must build itself tunnels of dried mud, hardened with its saliva, through which to travel from place to place; a creature which, without making a visible hole, can progress through the soil anywhere; a creature which will eat anything—except metals—that comes in contact with the ground. This pest, the termite, in Africa will rise under the paraffined canvas floor of one's tent, which it cannot penetrate, and at dead of night give voice to its wrath by an eerie, rhythmic pulsation, which startles and bewilders the newcomer. I doubt whether any-one knows how it produces the succession of droning vibrations. In the morning, when the tent is removed, not a vestige—not a suggestion—of a hole is to be discovered, not a shadow of explanation of the enigma remains.

One wonders sometimes why the whole continent of Africa does not crawl into the sea! Africa, which many people conceive of as densely wooded, has, in reality, little forest. This is due largely to the widespread agricultural activities of the very large population, but also to those same termites, which, however, do not seem to interfere with cultivation.

It was an endless delight to stroll in Africa—to stroll anywhere. Here on the trunk of a tree is a chameleon—the most preposterous and unbelievable beast, with two spike horns extending out in front—a veritable monster in miniature—apparently harking back a hundred mil-

lion years to a giant cousin, the terrific horned Tricera-
tops. Most of him was lettuce-green a moment ago; now
he is rapidly becoming a metallic purple-brown. However, a bit of him turns sky-blue and another bit vermilion. He is about ten inches long, and his legs jut out
from his body at sharp angles, and he has two toes on
each foot, each toe having two nails. His eyes, large,
prominent globes covered with scales, minute perfora-
tions for pupils, roll about, each eye independent of the
other. One may be looking forward while the other
looks backward—a vastly more practical arrangement
than ours. These eyes move on a universal joint, and
may be focused in any direction—up, down, at an angle;
one eye follows all your motions, while the other measures the distance between the chameleon and a fly several
inches away. Suddenly the tongue shoots out and returns with the fly sticking to the tip, but the creature
never takes one eye off you!

Here is a troop of sixty or seventy mongooses, the
size of half-grown cats, short-legged, gray-and-black-
banded. They dart to the crest of a little naked mound
and abruptly sink out of sight. You find, upon investigation, they have dived into an anthill. The clay of this
hill, a different color from the surface clay, has been
brought up from ten or fifteen feet below, mixed with
the saliva of the ants, and is almost as hard as stone. The
top of the low mound is punctured by a dozen or more
perpendicular openings, some of them six or eight inches
across. There was not an ant in sight. Why? What had
become of them all? Possibly they had been disposed of
by the ant-eating aardvark, which draws them out of their

The aardvark or earth pig

nests by suction, making a loud, raucous noise, which I was told may frequently be heard at night.

Then there is the rhinoceros beetle—a huge black fellow, bearing on his head an upright, half-inch horn. What does he do with it? Does he spit his enemies on it? His neck looks neither long nor flexible enough to make any use of his weapon. Why was he provided with it?

This rock has splits and crevices, edges of which suggest tenancy. So I explore by inserting my long slender switch, with the result that a series of tiny squeaks and gnashings of minute teeth become audible. I renew my gougings, and a bat emerges. Despite the blinding sunlight, he flaps an uneven way to the nearest tree, where no doubt he knows of a better 'ole.

Here are grasshoppers as big as hummingbirds; they fly at man's approach and travel a half-mile before settling down again. Here are little stunted thornbushes that look like decrepit dwarf trees. Conspicuous along their stems are black globes, like large marbles. These are not fruit, but swellings caused by the sting of a very small ant, which makes its abode inside. There are acres, miles of these thinly scattered bushes, which struggle to sustain life while the intruding parasites swarm up and down their stems.

The African tick is the most extraordinary I ever saw. It infests the long grass in incredible numbers. I never ceased to marvel as I observed the way this creature climbs to the top of a grass stem, and, on the approach of some animal, exhibits its wonderful intelligence and skill. It clings to the stem with the set of legs on one side of its body, while the legs on the opposite side are lifted free, ready to take hold of the animal at the first opportunity. Behind him on the grass stem will be four or five more ticks lined up in a row, awaiting their turn. Their feet are marvels of adaptability, and, as for beauty, every tick is artistically marked in white and brown patterns, intricate, harmonious, ingenious. They constitute a serious problem for animals, who have no way of getting rid of them, but a man can deal with them easily. All you have to do is to remove all clothing every night, and, using a flashlight and your hands, search your whole body methodically. If there is a tick on you anywhere, you can readily detect it, as it takes some hours for the insect to work its way through the skin. But if a single one ever penetrates, there is always danger of a possibly serious infection.

There were no mosquitoes at Lukenia, and very few flies, but there were quantities of other insects. You met them in the most unexpected places.

As I wrote in my tent one night, with the door still open, a large pale-green praying mantis appeared on my table and examined me with intense curiosity. He turned his flat, triangular head from side to side deliberately, fixed his enormous globular eyes on me, and put out his two long forefeet to feel the edge of my paper. Apparently I was the queerest object he had ever run into. When I put out a finger to him, he shrank back dubiously; but after further inspection he decided to accept my invitation, and walked up on my hand, his clawed green feet tickling my skin. I put him on the wall of the tent, and he hung there, upside down, as he continued to study me with unassuaged interest. His trustfulness was touching.

47

The memory of these early carefree days at Lukenia is very pleasant. We had been there for about a month when a native arrived with a message, saying that Mr. Pomeroy, with the rest of the Eastman party, would arrive at Nairobi the following day. Mr. and Mrs. Akeley, in their Buick, started immediately for Nairobi to meet them. After some days the Akeleys returned, with Rockwell. The Eastman party, we were told, had gone out into the Rift Valley to hunt.

Akeley had scarcely arrived at camp when I felt that something was not quite right. Although I asked no questions, I saw that he was perturbed, anxious. His happy air of successful accomplishment was gone. During the days that followed, it became clearer that something was preying on his mind. He did not shoulder his rifle and start off buoyantly each morning; he didn't chat so gaily at mealtimes.

We were at Lukenia about six weeks. During this time I finished my main study for the klipspringer group and painted a number of supplementary studies—cloud shadows, rock lichens, vegetation, etc., as guides. Jansson, meanwhile, had executed a wealth of accessory studies. All this work done by the two of us was the property of the Museum. Akeley wanted the Museum to have a gallery in which to house art studies made in the field. He planned to have them among the Museum's permanent exhibits, as permanent records and as sources of information for scientists and artists.

Toward the end of May we began to wind up our work and prepare to leave Lukenia. We were all sorry to go.

Chapter V

The Waso Nyiro

FROM LUKENIA WE JOURNEYED NORTH, for three hundred miles, toward the frontier of Kenya Colony, to what is called, in Mrs. Akeley's book, *Carl Akeley's Africa,* the Northern Waso Nyiro.

To get there we had to travel past the peaks of Mt. Kenya and through portions of its vast primeval forests. In this poet's paradise I saw a band of long-tailed monkeys, about the size of fox terriers, traveling single file. The first one I saw was running out to the end of a lofty bough of a large tree, and as the bough swung downward, the monkey leaped fully ten feet through the air and caught a slender sapling. His weight bowed the sapling far over, and as it swayed he leaped from it and caught the limb of another tree. Meanwhile, as the released branch of the first tree swung up, a second monkey ran out on it; the limb again bent, and this animal leaped just in time to catch the sapling as it snapped back, freed from the first monkey's weight. The second acrobat sent the sapling again switching far over and left it just in time to meet the downward swing of the second bough the first monkey had abandoned. One after another, in the most perfect timing trapeze acrobats ever dreamed of, some fifteen animals passed swiftly before my spellbound eyes.

49

In this incredible fashion monkeys travel across mile after mile of the vast forest.

Akeley told me that once as he stood facing the open sky at the edge of a cliff in this region, a band of these monkeys began springing from the bough of a tree over his head, passing across his vision to land on the flat resilient top of another tree far below. He estimated the leap at a hundred feet. Each monkey, as he flew through the air, used his tail somewhat in the manner of a rudder.

Incredible? No. Nothing is incredible in these fabulous forests. Here are trees of Gargantuan proportions, gemlike lakes, hidden and remote; wild, unexplored canyons. Superstitious fears and inadequate weapons prevent the natives from penetrating these fastnesses, so that they remain an untouched field for science and romance. They are traversed by hundreds of game trails that no man has ever followed, and offer adventure without end. Elephant, buffalo, rhinoceros, hippopotamus, lion, leopard, chimpanzees, Calabus monkeys, and many other creatures swarm there, in an undisturbed state of nature such as exists on few parts of the earth's surface today. I counted thirty-seven ostrich in one band we saw, and the zebra could be computed only by thousands.

We had to ford the Waso Nyiro River, a rapid, muddy stream, about two feet deep and a hundred feet wide, running through a semidesert country. There was evidence of a former bridge which had been washed away.

Five miles beyond the river, beside the dry bed of a tributary stream, we made camp in a grove of acacia trees. We were now at the end of our trek, having pene-

Grevy's hybrid in Tanganyika

trated to not very far south of Abyssinia, on the ancient caravan route which leads from that former African kingdom far down into equatorial Africa. No one knows how old this trail is—certainly many thousands of years —yet it is still a well-used road for camels. Millions of slaves have been carried over that old road, and it is said that the trade still goes on.

At the point where the caravan trail crossed the dry stream, there was a stone-lined well some thirty feet deep, which gave us a plentiful supply of good water.

The trees about us were woven together by vines which were often as big round as a man's thigh, and resembled writhing serpents. In some places they sprawled on the clean, dry sand, as if frozen in twisted attitudes of agony. At other points they climbed, with ferocious energy, up the staggering trees, their cables crippling and deforming the limbs, then cascading down again to leap up still other trees from which they dangled in huge loops and hangman's nooses. They were called monkey vines, for what reason I have no idea.

Mwanika, our temperamental cook from Nairobi, made his kitchen in the midst of these outlandish monstrosities, using what resembled the humped-up back of a petrified anaconda to hang his dishcloths on, and propping his flour sack against a gargoyle near by.

The sand by the Waso Nyiro was a golden pink-tan, and the rocks a greenish faded sky blue—marvelous combination! The bushes all about us were armed with thorns. Everything in the nature of vegetation had its thorn. I never dreamed there was such a variety of thorns on the earth. *"Mwiba,"* my gun boy called them. Sounds innocent, doesn't it? But as you moved about you soon instinctively avoided touching tree, bush, or shrub, whenever possible. You sensed gradually that here, in this semidesert, the struggle for survival was grim, terrific. Only vegetation that could defend itself against the onslaughts of ravenous herbivores could escape extermination. We had come to a giant thorn exposition. There were thorns six inches long, and thorns so small that they constituted merely a vicious fuzz. There were thick thorns and slender thorns, straight and curved thorns, single thorns and branching thorns. One tree sheds its bark annually, but never its thorns. Consequently, an oval disk of bark surrounding each thorn remains, and year after year is augmented by the bark renewing itself beneath, until the accumulated disks form bumps or warts an inch and a half high, with the original thorn, its strength enhanced by age, protruding from the top.

To the uninitiated the word "desert," or even "semidesert," calls up visions of desolation, sand dunes, bleaching bones, stifling heat. There was nothing like that in the Waso Nyiro. It was not hot because it was not humid. It was not dismal, but radiant and vibrating with light; not desolate, but crowded with life; and as for the bones, I saw none there. Although we were there in the dry season, the whole land was strewn with colors. The grasses were every shade of green, buff, canary, and pearl gray; the clay was old rose, pink; the sand saffron. Scattered everywhere were conical anthills, anywhere from three to ten feet high, and these were maroon red, having been carried up, grain by grain, from an underlying stratification of oxide-of-iron-stained clay. The flowers were orange and lemon, ver-

milion, blue, white, purple, and carmine. They dotted
the plains, and here and there strange awkward trees,
without leaves, were covered all over with brilliant red
blossoms.

It all reminded me strongly of the Painted Desert in
Arizona. Here were the rock-ribbed lilac mountains
against a lavender-cerulean sky, bathed in scintillating
light except where purple cloud shadows floated down
their slopes; here were the same flimmering heat waves
and little spiral dust devils, the blue retreating distances
fading into an infinitely delicate palpitating haze. But
the contours of these mountains were entirely different
from those of Arizona. Instead of being flat-topped
mesas, these were jagged, uptilted fragments of broken
earth crust. I painted them for the water-hole group.

Those rocks which lie in the bottom of the river have
been eroded through millions of years of grinding by
flood-driven silt and sand. They are blue limestone, and
the stratifications have been tilted by seismic action to
an almost perpendicular position. In the bed of the
stream these upstanding masses have been ground down
until only a few of them are visible, but if the covering
sand were removed, there would appear a succession of
pockets cut in the softer parts of the rock, while below
these the harder parts remain—barriers over which the
flood waters must flow. When the freshets of the rainy
season have passed, these pockets retain water-soaked
sand—water that cannot escape, and the dry sand above
it prevents the water from evaporating.

The moving water of the river is full of mud, salt, and
alkali, so that the animals will not drink it; but in these
pockets it is strained clear, and to these the beasts

crowd. The herbivorous animals come to drink about noon; the carnivores at night. The former sometimes locate water spots amid expanses of dry sand, apparently by scent, and reach it by digging with their front feet. In some places the water rises above the sand, but usually it has to be excavated.

When the dry season is at its height and the steady sunshine has sucked dry every water pan and unprotected rock pocket, the river becomes the only source of water, and the river bed becomes the resort of beasts flocking there from the adjacent plains and hills. The haunts of some are so far that hours of travel, back and forth, are necessary each day.

In my painting for the water-hole group the floodwater bed of the Waso Nyiro is shown at this season. The river, four feet down in its trough, is not visible to the observer, but its course is marked by the line of acacia trees off toward the base of the mountain. There is now a bridge at this point, and Martin Johnson had a landing field and camp site on the far side. On the new, improved road, people drive up from Nairobi in one day, and the spot has become something of a picnic ground. The animals, however, have all abandoned this water hole, for the picnickers made a practice of shooting them as they came to drink!

The natives in this region, the Samburu, locate water by thrusting long sticks into the sand of the dried-up stream bed. On the surface all is as dry as tinder, but the stick sunk into the sand discovers the pocket, and when a deep, extensive subterranean pool is found, the Samburu excavate a rude well, six to ten feet deep, until they reach water. They put a fence of felled thornbushes around the well, these forming a barrier no animal will attempt to force. Just outside this fence they place a long trough hollowed out of a log, and a smaller trough extends from the well through the fence, so that buckets of dipped water can conveniently be poured into the drinking trough.

A man gets into the well. He has nothing on but a breechclout, and he dips water with the rhythmic regularity of a machine; his ebon body, wet and moving, gleams like polished bronze, and the play of muscles is grand to behold. As soon as the man is seen approaching the well with his bucket, the thirsty domestic animals surge forward in a dense mob: cattle, camels, donkeys, sheep, goats, all pushing, panting, and fighting. Boys and girls from ten to eighteen, naked to the waist, stand about armed with stout sticks to enforce order.

Because the camels are the biggest and strongest, they are given first chance at the trough. The glistening dipper works might and main, but the camels constantly suck the trough dry, and those farthest away fight those nearer for a chance at the water. The battles become so fierce that the boys and girls have to take a hand, their sticks whacking and banging on bony skulls and tough shoulders; only when the blows come in showers do they make any impression. The insatiable camels filled at last, the cattle get their drink, while the calves are beaten back and made to await their turn, lest they be crippled in the melee. The native cattle—even the calves—habitually are treated with such kindness that they have no fear, and only the most persistent pounding with sticks can influence them. After the cattle come the donkeys, then the colts and calves, lastly the goats and sheep.

Despite the milling of the thirsty beasts, not much dust arises from the sand in the dry stream bed. The mongrel dogs of the natives sit on the neighboring blue rocks, and look on, philosophically awaiting their turn.

The Samburu have very large herds of cattle, and as they do not till the soil, their chief occupation consists in tending these herds. The herder carries a long slender spear with a leaf-shaped head of the ordinary elongated pattern; the spear is not heavy enough for serious fighting, and serves quite another purpose. When a lion or leopard approaches, the herder uses this spear as a discourager. He holds it in front of the marauder, but carefully refrains from touching him, knowing that if touched, the great cat would attack and kill him. He heads off, bothers, and generally confuses and disgusts the feline, until it turns away contemptuously, seeking less troublesome game.

In the evening, the herders sing at the top of their voices while their great flocks of cattle, sheep, and goats are being brought into thorn corrals for the night. This vocalization effectively discourages the carnivores.

The corral is circular, and in the center is a small round hut built of strong poles sunk in the ground, plastered with clay, and roofed. This retreat not only shelters the herder at night; it also constitutes an isle of safety around which the defeated may escape when the great bulls battle with one another at night. Again, when lions roar outside the thorn fence, the cattle huddle in terror on the opposite side of the corral. This leaves the side toward the lion empty, and the cat may hesitate, in its running around the outside of the fence, and cause the cattle to shift their position in a wild

Native interfering with a lion that has leaped into his corral

seething jumble. Sometimes two or three lions circle the corral in opposite directions, occasioning within an indescribable chaos and turmoil of milling brutes. But since the gate of the corral has been closed with thorns, one or more of the lions must eventually vault the fence, to get at the cattle.

If it is only one lion, the herder, seeking his opportunity in the wild confusion, springs between the lion and the herd, and interferes with his spear. Sometimes he is killed. Sometimes the lion disregards him, especially if a second lion leaps the fence at a different point. If the lion is alone, he may become disgusted at being interfered with, and leap out of the corral again without having done more than create excitement. The leopard rarely attacks cattle in this way; he prefers smaller game.

We placed our water-hole group in the country of the Samburu, who belong to the great Masai race. The Samburu had a village about a mile from our camp. I was the first to discover it. Alone that day, I had been following the bed of the dry tributary to the Waso Nyiro, watching a band of green monkeys who kept to the fringe of trees that skirted the stream. Retreating before me, they led me to a point where I could see a gently sloping hillside, on which a thorn corral surrounded a little group of beehive huts. Only their rounded tips appeared over the fence, however, and I went forward, intent on seeing more. I went around the corral, passing on my way a crippled dog which lay in the shade and looked up at me hopelessly; I finally found the entrance on the opposite side.

The village consisted of some thirty or forty of the

beehive huts made of switch wicker and mud, reinforced with skins. In such dwellings it is not possible to stand erect, and one had to enter on hands and knees. There were plenty of women about. Each Samburu has from three to four wives, and there is no law against having more. Near one hut some women sat chatting as they cleaned the pulp from pumpkin seeds which they afterward put in flat baskets to dry in the sun. Numerous naked children wallowed in the dust or scampered about. A mangy tortoise-shell cat sniffed disgustedly at the discarded pumpkin-seed pulp. A hen with chicks bustled importantly about, and a red rooster was busy capturing a grasshopper, which he ungallantly devoured himself without calling the hens. The women began to joke about me in their own language, and the children stopped romping to stand staring, with open mouths. Other women stood up to look over the tops of huts or peeped out of doorways. Several emaciated curs, lying in narrow strips of shade beside the huts, or searching in rubbish heaps for bones, looked at me. One or two emitted languid barks but soon stopped: it was too much effort. I shortly ceased to be a sensation, and went on investigating the metropolis unheeded.

But where were the men of the village? I could not see one. I learned later that all were out with their herds at this time of the day.

The huts were arranged according to no plan, haphazardly. Flies were abundant, and such flies as are encountered only in Africa—damnable flies! They alighted joyously on my face, neck, throat, and ears, and walked about with a deliberate persistence that would put Lucifer's imps to shame. A gang of fifteen or twenty of these flies will follow a man all day, and I discovered only one way of getting rid of them: to kill them off, one by one, methodically, with a persistence as relentless as their own. It takes an hour or more to exterminate twenty flies, and demands the utmost cunning and a ruthless ferocity, but it is the only alternative to many hours of torment.

There is a good reason for the hellishness of African flies. The natives believe, as do the Egyptian fellahin, that the spirits of man's ancestors live on in beasts, birds, reptiles, and insects. Therefore it is impious to shoo away flies, since in so doing you may be annoying the venerable spirit of your grandmother or your great-grandfather.

This superstition may account largely for the prevalence of blindness in Africa, as mothers allow flies to crawl freely on babies' faces, sucking the moisture from their eyes and infecting them with malignant bacteria. In Egypt, the English have striven to stamp out this curse, but what can science accomplish among such people in the face of priestcraft?

As I went through the village fighting flies, I saw a hut before which a war spear was fixed in the ground. The war spear, unlike the herder's spear, is made entirely of beautifully wrought iron, save for a hand-piece of wood in the center where the weapon balances. One end of the spear is a two-edged blade three feet long, and the other end is a rounded spike of equal length. The war spear is always thrown at an enemy, and even at fifty feet its weight will carry it into any animal, even an elephant, up to the hand-piece.

This spear sticking upright in the ground before the

hut had a definite significance. The Samburu have a police system. The bravest and fittest young men of the tribe are selected to range their territory constantly to keep order. The plan recalls the old European system of knight-errantry. As the Samburu use no money in any form, they pay this police force in privileges. When a policeman comes to a village he selects whichever hut he prefers, and drives the spike end of his spear into the ground before the door. From that instant the hut and everything in it, wives included, becomes his for as long as he elects to remain. The man of the family immediately absents himself and remains outside the thorn corral as long as the spear stands before his door. If he makes the slightest objection, or comes inside the thorn fence before the spear is removed, the policeman is authorized to run him through.

While I stood looking at the spear, the policeman emerged from the hut carrying four additional weapons of the same kind, and a shield. He was a splendidly set-up stalwart, naked above the waist, and from the waist to a little below the knee he was wrapped in a clay-and-oil-treated skin. His hair was anointed with the same red clay and oil, and hung in little ropes. In front it was cut in a neat bang, square across the forehead, a half-inch above the eyebrows; behind it was gathered and tied in a knot.

A Samburu policeman never greets or salutes anyone; he would die rather than incline his head the fraction of an inch in recognition of a stranger—but he may smile. My policeman smiled, and I smiled.

I said, *"Uhalegani?"* (How are you?), and he said, *"Mzuri sana"* (I am very well).

I pointed to my camera, and held out a shilling; he accepted the shilling with dignity, and I took two snaps of him.

After looking the town over I went out by another gate in the thorn fence, and near it under an acacia tree found two men playing a game. One of them was old, the other about forty. I guessed him to be the dispossessed husband, the other his father. Both were nearly naked. The two were much engrossed in their game, which was something like backgammon. They moved pebbles about in pockets carved in a piece of wood, but there were apparently no stakes. I have seen the same game played with simple holes in the ground. I could not see where these two outcasts expected to live, but probably off in the bush somewhere they had a brush hut, as partial protection against the weather and the hyenas, which have a ghastly habit of biting a sleeper in the face.

The next day I came back to the village with my painting materials and my boy Ibrahim to paint a study of some of the huts. All afternoon, with my shining Mannlicher on his shoulder, Ibrahim marched up and down behind me, feeling enormously important, and tremendously impressive to the budding belles of the village who gathered in tittering groups to whisper and admire.

Samburu women came every day to our camp to trade milk for corn meal with our porters, and the haggling that went on was wonderful to listen to and observe. The porter tried to make the measuring cup hold as little as possible by putting in the meal loosely; the watching Samburu lady insisted on its being packed tight and heaped high. They wrangled and disputed, cheating, calling names, taunting, ridiculing. I listened in on one such argument, when one porter, called a "baby" because he had protested the quality of the milk he had received, retorted with such vicious eloquence that the lady found but one reply. She grabbed the nipple of another woman and squirted milk at him, whereupon everybody laughed.

These Samburu women have almost no hips, but very large posteriors. Judged by our standards, they are unesthetic specimens.

Chapter VI

The Water-Hole Group

OUR WATER-HOLE GROUP in the Museum features the giraffe; the cow is drinking at a water hole in the sand; the rest of the animals stand waiting, the most formidable of them nearest, ready to take their turn after the giraffe have finished. In the distance a group of elephant have a hole to themselves, and rhinoceros are trying to locate another hole. A couple of eland have finished drinking; a band of baboons is at an open pool among the rocks. The zebra are just arriving. Besides these groups appear impala, gerenuk, oryx, wild pig, Grant's and Thomson's gazelle, jackal, green monkeys, vultures, and marabou stork. In the trees are the nests of weaverbirds. In the foreground are desert quail. On a little hillside at the right of the group, the vultures are holding high revel where some animal has died. Each for itself in snatching at the bloody banquet, the loathsome birds gang together to beat off the jackals that try to get a share. Dust rising from the clayey hillside veils the ferocious battle.

Our chief concern in this group was the giraffe. We had decided that the big bull for the group must be fully sixteen feet high, to break our horizon line effectively. He must be dark as to color, his spots almost black; he must have large horns. A hunting party left camp every morning to find him, and one day I got up at four-thirty and went along. We traveled across the plain in a truck and finally climbed a small mountain, raking the country with our field glasses. We saw plenty of giraffe cows and calves, but no bull. The bull-giraffe question began to get serious. We had to have one.

Of all incredible creatures on this earth, none surpasses that which is sometimes suggestively called the camelopard. At first glance he suggests a grotesque form of Jurassic and Cretaceous life—the long-necked Brontosaurus. There is one definite similarity: the Brontosaurus developed his long neck by reaching up for air from the bottom of lakes, and the giraffe by stretching up to browse on tall trees. He developed his tall, disproportionate front legs in the same way. He is probably the most fantastic example of adaptation extant. Once, doubtless, he was a much smaller animal, with a moderately short neck and horns fit for self-defense. Perhaps then he expressed his emotions vocally, as do other creatures.

Somehow, somewhere, in the remote past, he developed the browsing habit, common to his family—the antelopes, for instance—in a peculiar form. He reached higher for his food, and altered his structure, by processes not easily understood, until he had at his command a food supply exclusively his own—he had no rivals, because no other could reach it.

But in the process of acquiring his monopoly he lost other advantages, as seems to be the rule. As his neck elongated, it lost its pushing power and fighting strength. That neck has now no vocal cords. The giraffe is the only voiceless animal. Where he once had not two, but three horns, and was probably a redoubtable fighter, he now has only vestigial remains—mere stumps covered with hide. His present defenses lie only in his sight, hearing, and speed. To these must be added his size and height. He is the tallest animal now on the earth, and his great velvety purple-black eyes can spy an enemy a long way off. Another of his achievements in adaptation is an extraordinarily long, sinuous tongue, which he can wind around an acacia switch, and, despite the thorns, strip off the feathery foliage.

His movement in action is unlike that of any other animal; whether walking, trotting, or galloping, he progresses with a rhythmic, undulating motion rippling throughout his whole body, like flowing water, and this gives him a distinguishing grace, compensation—as it were, for his ill-proportioned form. Later, in Tanganyika, I saw a line of these creatures walking along the crest of a long hill, single file, silhouetted against a sunset sky—the sight will never fade from my memory.

I never have heard of giraffe bulls fighting each other. I don't think they do; but they are capable of inflicting considerable damage by kicking forward or sideways with their front feet. Sir Samuel Baker records having come upon two lions fighting a giraffe, but I think such instances must be very rare indeed. The giraffe is powerful and fleet—no easy prey. Lions find many other animals easier to capture.

Nevertheless, one of the giraffe bulls we got had the claw marks of a lion on his flank—old scars. That would have been a strange fight to witness! Perhaps two or three lions attacked, snarling and growling, while our giraffe fought for his life in absolute silence.

We had come to this part of Africa because it contained the finest specimens of the giraffe. Akeley put in more than a week exploring the neighborhood for twenty miles to look all the animals over. It is very difficult to judge of the size of a giraffe; they all look gigantic, and when you see them singly it is exceedingly hard to tell which are the largest. The method Akeley adopted was to compare visually the bull with the tree nearest it, and, when the animal had gone, measure his height on the tree. By this means we finally selected a magnificent male, brought him down, and carried him into camp. Thereafter, Akeley, Rockwell, and Raddatz, along with a number of natives, were busy for about four days getting the pelts in shape. A female and a calf were soon procured as well, all of which involved a tremendous amount of labor. The work was done in the best shade that could be found, with a wagon sheet stretched overhead to help out.

The porters were free to take as much giraffe meat as they wanted, but it was not popular. They said it was tough, strong, and coarse. A large quantity of refuse therefore remained to be disposed of, and in Africa this always means placing it where it will be found by carrion eaters. For several days consecutively a pile of this giraffe meat lay on the far bank of the dry stream, and every night a struggling gang of ruffian scavengers congregated. Jansson, Rockwell, and I had our tents near each other, not more than fifty yards away from the scene of this gathering.

I maintain that neither the human nor any other vocal apparatus on earth can rival that of the hyena for poignant expressiveness. When these ravenous mobs of incarnate gluttony got going, they provided a more appalling

Hyenas fighting over offal with leopard joining in

sound picture of hell's fiends than the imagination of man could ever conceive. The roars, growls, squawks, squeals, hisses, wails, shrieks, groans, coughs, bawls, brays, whinnies, cackles, snickers—more sounds than there are English words to express—emitted nightly by these beasts, were absolutely unique in my experience. Rancor, venom, exasperation, blind rage, demoniacal fury, malignant spite, rabid expostulation, sizzling defiance, and frenzied despair—all were jumbled in a maelstrom of fantastic, jibbering bedlam, a screeching pandemonium—an unbelievably diabolical symphony of hate. By the sounds I could almost see what I knew was going on. The beasts were piled in a writhing heap, gouging, snapping, ripping, some with their heads buried to the ears in flesh and nearly smothering as they gnawed, while others tore at their hind quarters; still others with jaws locked in ghastly duels, or slicing and strangling each other; some being gutted. It was a cyclone of bestiality.

No one who has not seen the spotted hyena in his native surroundings can understood what I say of him, or even believe it. This creature lives chiefly in holes in the ground but also uses rock crevices. He prefers the earth holes because they are cooler, I imagine, or less favorable to the accumulation of vermin. However, the hyena does not dig these dens—he isn't able to; he usurps holes excavated by wart hogs. The usurper backs down into the oblique tunnel so that he faces the exit and any would-be intruder. He has rather long, sparse, wiry brindle hair, and as he backs into his narrow hole this hair gets pushed up the wrong way. Since he remains in the tube all day, only emerging about an hour before sundown, the ruffed-up hair becomes set permanently askew, especially along his spine and on his rump. This ragged, disheveled coat gives the beast a loutish and clownish appearance most unusual among the wild animals. Nature did not endow the hyena with grace, either. He emerges ridiculously from his den each evening, ungainly, shabby, lugubrious, with a grouchy and dyspeptic air. His expression is vacuous; his gait is a

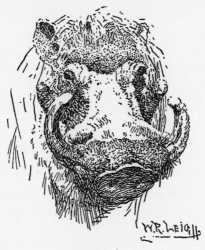

Wart hog

slow, clumsy walk. If he must hurry he proceeds in lumbering leaps, but he cannot run fast. His sad eyes have the glassy look of those we see in dead fish, or of the greasy rings that form on oily water in a stagnant harbor. I never saw him sprightly or gay, and he is almost always alone.

In spite of all this, the hyena can laugh. Yes, indeed, I have heard him. His laugh is the most dreadful sound you may ever hear on this earth. It expresses neither merriment nor joy but terrified perplexity; for he laughs when he is cornered or startled, and the sound is horrible, like the cachinnation of a maniac. When on the prowl, he occasionally lets out a wail pitched on the most dismal note conceivable, and expresses his outraged feelings, his disgust and despair. Altogether, the hyena is a kind of nightmare joke. I have lain on my cot listening to him and laughed until my pillow was wet.

This is what I was doing one night when suddenly a new kind of hell broke loose. I listened intently and came to the conclusion that some other animal had interrupted the giraffe-meat feast. Lion or leopard? Soon I caught a sound like a stick scraped across slats. I had heard that once from a leopard in a zoo. As a matter of fact, it was a leopard. Rockwell got out with his rifle, and by the light of the moon placed a shot that did the trick. The cat charged, as it does invariably when wounded, but dropped dead in the middle of the stream bed.

Nobody wastes sympathy on the hyena. He is a ghoulish brute. Among his ingratiating traits is his ability to discover when a female of any of the herbivores is about to give birth. He will follow her about, knowing she is not in a condition to elude him, and if there are no bulls present to fight him off, when the critical moment arrives, the hyena tears the cow to pieces.

In the part of Africa where we were, the hyena never attacks human beings, unless they are asleep. Akeley told me that one night, on a former trip, he happened to wake up and look out the door of his tent. In the moonlight he saw a hyena about to tear the face of a sleeping porter. Akeley grabbed his gun and fired, and the beast, emitting his horrible laugh, made off.

Hyena

I have been assured that the hyena's jaws, in spite of his far smaller size, are as strong as those of the lion. But he has no lion's heart. He is an arrant coward and possesses not a single admirable characteristic.

The grisly scavengers prevalent in this region included black vultures, Egyptian vultures, and griffon vultures. The marabou stork was another. Observing any of these creatures, it is easy to understand the classical invention of the harpy, which preyed upon and carried off the souls of the dead.

The hideous naked head and neck of the griffon vulture, rising from a white collar, and its ponderous and slouchy walk; the revolting bald cranium of the collared and caped black vulture; the ridiculous splotched and mangy pate, the preposterous beak and pendulous pouch of the horrific marabou stork, make one's blood creep with growing disgust, which returns as nightmare visions.

The marabou is also known as the adjutant stork, because of the military suggestion in its measured walk. It is an appropriate name. There is something pompous and austere, something clownishly martial, in the creature's strut. He is slopping over with importance; he is a superlative stuffed shirt.

These nauseous birds roost in bare, dead trees during the day, sitting motionless for hours, dark and heavy against the sky. They are about the size of a turkey, and at least twice as heavy as our buzzard. They also favored certain places on the ground, one an open acre where the caravan trail crossed the river. Here, for no apparent reason, they would congregate and walk aimlessly about in their ungainly fashion. Sometimes they would

W.R.LEIGH;

Griffon vulture

get into fights, and beat up the dust in clouds with their wings. Possibly they were attracted by scraps of meat scattered by the camel drivers, who camped near the well, but I never saw any scraps.

The water pan, of which I painted a study for the water-hole group, was about a mile away from our camp. When we first arrived, early in June, the water was rapidly disappearing, and the zone of mud surrounding it bore each morning a fresh record in the form of tracks; giraffe, rhinoceros, eland, oryx, impala, lion, hyena, and many more. Several trees stood near, and on one, a large colony of weaverbirds, which always build near water, had heavily loaded the branches on one side with their nests. Each nest hung from the extreme tip of a long drooping switch, and was so placed to prevent climbing snakes and egg-eating mongoose from reaching the nests.

The pool of water in the pen contracted more each day and became more muddy and foul, yet native women came daily to it to fill their gourds.

Every morning a truck took me out to location, came for me at noon, and brought me back in the afternoon. There was something thrilling about being out painting in that wild solitude. The heat was just sufficient to make the paint work beautifully without any thinning medium. To sit there painting in the vast shimmering landscape was ideal. My gun boy would sit and watch, and I wondered what was going on in his Abyssinian brain. Was he making unfavorable comparisons between what I was doing and the paintings he had seen in churches in Ethiopia? Questions were vain. Ibrahim's already wide lips would spread in a tremendous grin, exposing red gums and white teeth—that was all. Had I been adept in the Swahili tongue, doubtless he could have told me many interesting things. Sometimes he would ramble about in the neighborhood, occasionally bringing back a chameleon, snail, or locust he had captured.

The sparkling air palpitated and danced in rhythmic waves over stretches of amber, pearl-gray, and lemon grassland—over sage-green, purple, and lilac scrub—over brush that was russet, red, orange, and silver. The light glimmered and pulsated. Huge grasshoppers sailed

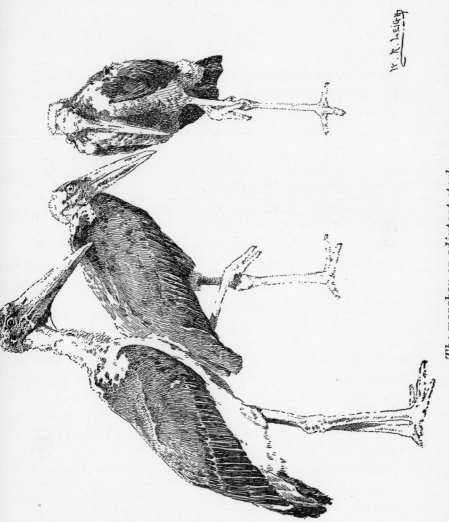

The marabou or adjutant stork

against the lavender shadow masses of the shrubs; velvet-black, saffron, white, and vermilion butterflies and moths frolicked from flower to flower. Off to one side spread a forest of acacias interspersed with other black-green growths with ash-gray stems. On all sides rugged mountain ridges formed a background, and above them were flecks of cloud and dark specks that were vultures against the cerulean fields. Sometimes Ibrahim would glide near, and pointing, whisper, *"Twiga!"* (giraffe) or it might be *"Punda milia!"* (zebra) or *"Kifaro!"* (rhinoceros). The small creatures came near—perhaps within a hundred feet, but not so the larger beasts. They remained from a quarter to a half-mile away, but were easily identified even at that distance.

As I painted away, reproducing doom palms and expanses of waterworn blue-gray rock, buff sand, and ocher grass, suddenly "Oho! Oho! Oho!" would come from behind, and I turned to glimpse a distant dark lump in the fork of a tree—an old-man baboon, *nyani,* telling me what he thought of me. With resounding cries hornbills would wing their way overhead, and unnamed songsters filled the air with melody.

The hornbill is worth considering. As I saw him, a heavy, ungainly black-and-white bird with a huge beak that seemed to need explanation, he was not beautiful; but I rather admired him. The hornbills make their nests in hollows that they excavate in trees. As soon as the female has laid two eggs she starts to set, and the male bird promptly walls up the opening with mud so she cannot get out. He leaves a narrow slit through which he feeds her faithfully. When the eggs hatch he opens the hole, she comes out, the aperture is again walled up, and the parents feed the nestlings through the opening. When the young hornbills are ready to fly, the nest is opened once more, and they come out.

Perhaps a family row among the green monkeys, *kima,* would get under way in some thicket not far off, and presently they would be racing through the tops of the trees. Again, a band of Thomson's gazelle might stray near, all innocent of any danger from the strange creature sitting under the umbrella. All the while, on the topmost branch of the tallest tree in the vicinity, one of the cast-iron marabou storks is keeping watch, convinced that but for his unremitting vigilance, this interloper would effect some evil treachery.

"Oho! Oho! Oho!" comes angrily from behind me. What he means would not be printable! "Oho! Oho!"

Chapter VII

The Black Buffalo

T HE AFRICAN BLACK BUFFALO is considered the most dangerous animal in the world. The bull, while not as big as some of our domestic bulls, is incredibly thick-set and muscular. He is nothing but muscles—huge muscles that are terrific in their power. Called the "black" buffalo, he is really black-brown, because he is nearly always dusty from dried mud, and his hair is thin in spots, where the hide shows through. At the shoulder he averages about five and a half feet high. Besides his compact, Herculean body, this buffalo has massy, wide-spread, curling horns. Not horns with points directed forward, like those of our domestic cattle, but weapons that extend out at right angles to his head. The buffalo knows how to use them with deadly efficiency. This is equally true of his hoofs.

Cattlemen know the vindictiveness displayed by the Alderney bull when enraged, and how he uses his hoofs if he gets a chance. Multiply the Alderney's ferocity several times, and you begin to approach that of the African buffalo. Anyone who has seen a fierce domestic bull pawing the ground with his front feet can fancy how, with similar hoofs, but with a vastly improved technique, the black buffalo tears his victim into shreds.

The black buffalo has no peer in relentless ferocity. He is the veritable incarnation of hatred—and in battle he is a master of diabolical craft. Yet it is neither his hoofs, his mighty strength, nor his deadly horns which make him the most frightful antagonist in the world: it is his vindictive cunning.

The black buffalo is widely distributed over Africa. He prefers swampy regions because he likes to wallow in mud, and swamps afford him the best cover. But since there are not enough swamps, he also inhabits forests and even bush country. The denser the growths the better he likes them, for in such jungles the advantages are all on his side. His senses—sight, smell, and hearing—are phenomenally acute, and upon suspecting the proximity of any other creature, he stands perfectly still, observing, waiting. His keen eyes are black and heavily lashed above, and as he gazes about he elevates his head above his shoulders. The huge muscles on his neck are more than eighteen inches through!

To illustrate his technique in the art of killing, and the unparalleled fervor he puts into it, let me recount three instances with which I am familiar.

An Englishman resident in Nairobi said that he once had met a black buffalo bull in a patch of forest, when he was out hunting with a friend. He was in the lead, and recognized his danger. Believing the bull would attack, and hoping to kill him first, the Englishman fired. But he only wounded the animal, which instantly charged. The Englishman jumped aside, but his leg was struck by a horn and broken. While the bull tore on to catch the second hunter, the first one, despite his broken leg, climbed a tree and got out on a branch, but his failing strength could carry him no higher. He could not even lift his injured leg, which dangled useless below the branch to which he clung. For over two hours he hung there, obliged to look on while the bull reduced his friend's body to fragments smaller than a half dollar. This accomplished, the animal turned his attention to the enemy in the tree. He could not reach him, but by taking a running jump he could hit the dangling foot with his horns, and thus amused himself for two hours more, jumping at and banging the foot. At last, perhaps weakened by his wound, the buffalo left, and the man was rescued by other hunters. He was able to walk with a crutch, at the time I heard the story, some years after the incident occurred.

The second case was that of my friend Will Richard, of Cody, Wyoming. He had an English guide. One evening while they were making camp in a country of open parks and bush patches, a large bull buffalo appeared about a hundred and fifty yards away, making for a thorn thicket. Richard caught up his rifle and fired. The bull lurched slightly, but went on into the bush. Because the wounded bull possessed an unusually fine set of horns Richard wanted to follow immediately, but his guide dissuaded him. Toward the evening of the next day, Richard proposed to enter the tunnel-like trail in search of the beast, thinking to find it dead. But the guide absolutely forbade his going in, insisting that the buffalo was *not* dead. By the third day, Richard was confident the animal certainly must have died, but again the guide vetoed any suggestion of going into the thorn-bush.

"Did you hear any lions last night?" asked the guide.

No, no lions had roared, except at a considerable dis-

The black buffalo

tance—far from the patch of thorn jungle into which
the wounded buffalo had gone.

"Do you see any vultures around?" asked the Britisher.

"No, no vultures!"

"That buffalo is still alive!" insisted the guide.

Richard offered the best hunter among their natives
five dollars to go into the bush and investigate. The
man, after considerable hesitation, consented. Wearing
nothing but a breech clout, and carrying his spear, the
African started into the covert. He moved by inches, so
cautiously that it took him more than an hour to cover
a hundred and fifty yards. Then he came to the edge of
an open space where the bull lay, apparently dead. For
nearly an hour the native watched, to see if he could
detect any signs of life, any breathing or twitching. Not
a sign. With infinite caution the man approached and
touched the bull with his spear. Instantly the beast
scrambled to its feet! The native fled down the thorn
alley, the bull after him. Halfway, realizing he would be
caught, the native leaped into the air and seized the
overhanging limb of a tree. The limb broke and the man
landed on the buffalo's rump. Rolling off behind, as the
bull turned around to the left he darted past it on the
right, and got safely out of the bush.

Though all this activity took place where the two
white men could hear every sound, they could not see
what was happening or get a chance to shoot at the bull,
which, of course, was too wise to come out of his cover.

The next afternoon there was another controversy.

"That bull hasn't had any water in four days!" argued
Richard. "He surely must be dead by now!"

"He isn't dead. No lions, or even hyenas, have gathered. No vultures have appeared. He's alive!"

Finally Richard announced his determination: he would go into the thorn to investigate.

"If you *will* go in, I'll go with you!" said the other.

They entered the bush cautiously and reached the open space: it was empty.

"He's gone—escaped!" cried Richard.

"He's not gone! Look out!"

At that instant the buffalo charged from his cover. The guide sprang behind a tree, jerking Richard after him, but not quite quickly enough. The bull's horn glanced from Richard's arm, and one flying hoof struck his leg, knocking him over into the thorns. The bull's charge carried him beyond the tree and before he could turn, the two men darted for safety. They escaped only because the weakened animal could not overtake them. That night there was no assemblage of lions or hyenas; the next morning there were no vultures.

"That buffalo is not going to die!" announced the Britisher, and they left the place.

A third episode occurred at the Tinga-tinga Mcubwa, the big swamp which is a famous haunt of the buffalo. The hired guides who conduct foreign hunters to the haunts of coveted game keep an eye on this swamp, for if the buffalo have remained unmolested for some time, the guides can take their patrons to the place in the late afternoon with some hope of finding the beasts out on the plains, grazing.

Under such conditions the Crown Prince of Sweden was once guided to the Tinga-tinga, where he wounded a big bull. The animal staggered into the marsh thickets, and the Prince was for following immediately to finish him off. His guide counseled against such a move, explaining why. The Prince insisted: he was not afraid. He entered the swamp, accompanied by the guide. They had penetrated the growths but a short distance when the hidden buffalo charged at close quarters, so close, in fact, that before the Prince could pull the trigger, the bull's head struck the rifle muzzle, and the butt of the weapon knocked the Prince over backwards. In the same split second the guide killed the bull. That the bullet dropped the buffalo in his tracks was a rare piece of good luck, for, barring a miracle, both men would have been dead in another two minutes.

While I was in Africa I heard considerable discussion among hunters and other informed people as to the relative deadliness of the great beasts. I discussed the subject with natives whenever I got a chance. From what I learned, and from my own observations, I came to the following conclusions, which I believe will be supported by facts and experience.

The black buffalo is generally conceded to rank first in point of danger to man. The elephant is second. Like the buffalo, he is vindictive and cunning, and extremely keen of scent and hearing, but he usually tries to avoid you, especially if he has not been hunted recently. The rhinoceros, if he sees you before he smells you, will run away, although if he scents you first within three hundred yards, he is apt to charge. He is the third in point of danger. From the cats, save in exceptional cases, there is practically no hazard between sunrise and a half-hour before sunset, but the animal fourth in deadliness is the leopard because, if wounded, he never fails to charge, and only death will stop him. The lion comes fifth. He is rather a gentlemanly killer, frequently leaving his victim before the latter is dead.

The natives fear the buffalo beyond any other animal, mainly because he will attack even when he is not being molested.

Travel in the great interior of Africa must be almost entirely on foot, as horses, mules, and donkeys are all killed by tsetse fly. Camels are hard to manage, and more expensive than human carriers. Therefore native porters are used. The roads they follow are usually mere footpaths, intended for single-file walking. Only in rare instances have the whites widened these trails to six feet, and this widening consists merely in cutting down the elephant grass, bamboo, or brush at the sides of the trail. It makes the traveling somewhat more agreeable but no more safe. Danger of attack by buffalo, elephant, or rhinoceros is forever present.

Bearing on their heads their fifty-pound loads, the porters move at a dogtrot, single file along the narrow trails. Often the long line of burden bearers of some safari will extend for half a mile. The instant there is an alarm of any sort, every porter flings his load to the ground and darts into the densest cover he can find.

But with walls of elephant grass twelve feet high on both sides, or in bush or jungle country, it is quite impossible for even the keen-sensed natives to tell in time whether a herd of buffalo has scented them and stampeded. Unsuspecting, the porters trot on, while a big bull buffalo leaves the stampeded herd, circles back, and comes into the trail behind the line. The first intimation the unfortunate men have of buffalo being in the vicin-

Buffalo attacking natives in the Congo

ity is when the bull rushes at them from behind, plowing
through their file, hurling them in every direction. Having executed this maneuver the bull does not tarry to
mutilate his victims, for he knows he is surrounded.
While the confusion is at its height, he plunges into
cover and makes off. Sometimes two bulls together will
play this trick.

It was early in July when Mr. and Mrs. Akeley,
Raddatz, and I left the camp by the caravan trail. To
carry our supplies and our native helpers, we took three
trucks and the light touring car, and these we had to get
across the ford at the Waso Nyiro River the same way
as when we came, with block and tackle and all hands
helping. We left Rockwell and Jansson to follow later.

We reached Meru the following day, at noon, and,
after having procured some supplies, we went on to
Embu, on the southeast slope of Mt. Kenya. That ride
through the foothills of Mt. Kenya I thought the most
beautiful I had ever taken in my life. Every turn
brought something new and thrilling. We would descend along the side of some deep ravine, dropping
deeper and deeper into the gloom of tropical forests,
until we neared the head of a ravine, where a bridge and
a sharp turn sent us climbing the opposite side up to the
high slopes, where we were surrounded by sunlit fields
of grain and the banana groves of the Kikuyu. Around
the point of the hill another descent was before us, and
this kept on all day. We sometimes traveled several
miles to make one in an air line.

Two or three days later we left Embu, going still farther south to Kagio, not far from the great swamp.

Kagio was the camp where we had spent the first night out from Nairobi on our way to the Waso Nyiro. We had completely encircled Mt. Kenya.

After several trips out from Kagio to look over the ground, we settled on a place for our camp, and moved over to the swamp, where I first was to become acquainted with *mbogo,* the black buffalo.

Mr. Eastman, Mr. Pomeroy, Dr. Stewart, their two English guides, Percival and Ayer, and also Mr. and Mrs. Martin Johnson arrived at the Tinga-tinga shortly before we got there. Our first camp was at what we called the upper end of the swamp, that is, the end from which the watershed ran down. It was the point first reached upon leaving Kagio on the main road. The Eastman party had tried for buffalo at Embu, but, finding none, had come on here. But getting buffalo here was also a hardy man's work, and way beyond a man of Eastman's physique and experience. Besides, to him, the place was uninteresting, and he did not like the mosquitoes. Nobody blamed him or was surprised when he and his party left for Tanganyika. Mr. and Mrs. Akeley, Raddatz, and I, with Rockwell and Jansson, who had now joined us, remained at the swamp, and we immediately moved to the lower end, where painting possibilities were better.

There was no trail to follow, only the open level of an ancient grass-covered lava flow—a ridge half a mile wide forming the eastern limit of the swamp. Depressed country lay on both sides. On our right, a hundred feet below us, were smooth, somewhat boggy plains retreating to low rolling hills covered sparsely with acacia scrub; on the left the swamp, about five miles long and three wide, was only twenty feet below us.

The Tinga-tinga Mcubwa was brought into existence many thousands of years ago by a tremendous eruption which blew off the top of Mt. Kenya, twenty miles away. The lava from that eruption streamed out like giant tentacles across the level grass plains, covering a vastly older flow, and dammed the beautiful Tana River. The obstructed river flooded some of the spaces between the lava tentacles, and so we have the Tinga-tinga Mcubwa —the great swamp. It is in reality a shallow lake, nowhere more than two feet deep, with the river flowing through it. The water, which flows over the lava bottom, is clear and fresh.

The swamp is covered everywhere with a dense matted growth generally some eight feet tall, gradually diminishing in height at the edges. I have never found anyone who could give a name for this growth, but it is very beautiful and covered with yellow blossoms. Akeley told me that when he first saw the swamp it was full of cattails, but now we found these entirely supplanted by the yellow growth.

The swamp provides perfect cover and absolute safety for the buffalo as long as he remains there, for neither man nor beast, unless uninformed or reckless of life, will attempt to follow him. But the buffalo cannot eat the swamp growth, and is obliged to come out for food. Excellent grass grows on the disintegrated black soil covering the lava flow, and about four o'clock every afternoon the herds, if left undisturbed, come out of the swamp to graze. If molested, they come out only at night.

Kavirondo crane

THE BLACK BUFFALO

Mr. and Mrs. Akeley had visited the place some time earlier, and picked out an isolated spot near the outlet of the swamp, from which I was to make my studies, and I was eager to begin.

Our three trucks bumped and creaked as they followed the touring car through the waist-high flower-dotted grass. Hundreds of quail scurried out of our way; an occasional duiker plunged across our course. A long-legged secretary bird craned his neck to appraise us with philosophic deliberation. On the marshy plains to the right a herd of zebra crowded about a water hole, while kongoni and impala waited their turn. Not far removed was a large congregation of Kavirondo crane making a great noise and flapping their wings, apparently holding a conclave of momentous import.

This crane is among the most beautiful birds in the world. I would like some wiseacre evolutionist to explain to me how nature came to design such an ornate and inexplicable creature. It has a pearl-gray, black, and brown body, a velvet-black head with white and red cheeks, and, most singular of all, an amber egretlike crest. Its cry is so loud that it can be heard even when it is invisibly remote overhead.

At one time certain helmets worn by units of the French army were each adorned with a Kavirondo crane crest, and as a consequence the birds were almost exterminated, like our Florida egret. But fortunately the military style has changed, and the crane are slowly becoming plentiful again.

Chapter VIII

The Tinga-tinga Mcubwa

OUR FIRST CAMP was located within a hundred and fifty feet of the swamp, at one of the few points where the lava rock was exposed. As we neared the site a lesser bustard rose from a clump of low bush and flapped away. Afterwards I found there an abandoned nest with twelve speckled eggs almost ready to hatch: a great pity. Dark green bushes and wild hollyhocks were scattered near the edge of the swamp. A hundred yards farther on, through a depression in the lava flow, a streamlet of water from the swamp ran across, cascading down on the far side in tiny leaps, and gliding amid lava boulders to the plains below. Two miles further on the Tana River broke over the lava flow in a succession of low cataracts and rapids, amid islands covered with tropical jungle, in a chaos of rocks, fallen trees, roots, vines, grass, flower masses, whirling pools, and white foam. Along the river were the tracks and wallows of hippopotamus and many signs of crocodiles.

It was a delightful spot—that camp, entirely open, with a fine view in every direction. There were few trees near us, and each of these stood isolated. They were all old, gnarled, twisted, and patriarchal. Strange fruit hung from the limbs of several. Yellowish apple-green, it was sometimes half a foot long, and resembled a huge sausage, hanging pendulumlike on a foot-long stem.

94

Every one of these ancient trees bore the scars of many wounds received from one source or another in the past. Every wound was recorded on the trunk, and around every one the tree had built up protecting ridges of live green bark. The limbs had been mercilessly

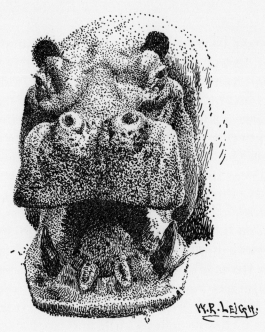

Hippopotamus

hacked and lopped off by natives in quest of firewood, yet clusters of new, vigorous shoots had sprung from the stumps. I couldn't help wondering how these maltreated trees continued to live, yet there they were, vigorous and hardy, clothed in handsome dark-green leaves, producing fine crops of their grotesque sausages to swing in the breeze. Amazing examples of perseverance, they recalled Byron's lines: "In the desert a fountain is springing; in the wide waste there still is a tree!"

Wonderful old trees! They were like men who have withstood the tempests of littleness, stupidity, meanness; men like Akeley, gaunt, hard as iron, standing unyielding for an idea, a big conception, against all that is petty, purblind, commonplace.

The larger trees had sections of hollow logs about two feet long, suspended horizontally among their branches —beehives, placed there by the natives. Sooner or later these log hives are found and inhabited by the swarms of wild bees we often heard passing overhead. Beyond this, bee culture is unknown, although honey (*asali ya nyuki*—sirup of the bee) is the only sweet the natives have, and is so precious that very stringent laws govern its collection and handling. Each man keeps tabs on his own hive, and if there is any pilfering the thief is killed.

Under each isolated tree there was a rank growth of grass, thanks to guano from the birds whose feet had polished many of the uppermost branches clean and shiny. They were hawks or eagles mostly, for in all these grass wastes they could find no other perch so safe. I rarely have approached one of these trees without seeing a bird of prey fly out of it.

Along the water's edge there were delightful open pools surrounded by six-foot walls of vegetation matted intricately together with slender vines and exuberant undergrowths. On the surface of these pools lay lacy sheets of floating vegetation, forming lettuce-green patches, and between them, on the dark brown-green water, floated lily pads and exquisite lavender lotus blossoms.

Covering the swamp extended an expanse of orange-

96

yellow blossoms, and in the distance a fitful line of dark trees marked the course of the Tana. Above the swamp, ridge on ridge, retreated undulating hills. Countless little wisps of smoke rose from these hills, each marking a Kikuyu fire where food was being cooked. Over these hills hung perpetually a mass of low-lying clouds, and above these rose the magnificent peak of Mt. Kenya, whose upper reaches have never been scaled.

The swamp, with all its beauty and interest, was terribly infested with a species of anopheles, the mosquitoes that transmit malarial fever. Against these pests we had tried to arm ourselves, our defenses consisting of boots, handkerchiefs tied around our heads, turned-up collars, and retreat into our tents as soon as darkness came on. But the bloodsuckers could bite through a woolen shirt, and as they did not stay near the ground boots did not help much. A favorite place of attack was the back of the neck. They were very canny mosquitoes, making little noise, and they were already active an hour before sunset. To avoid them, therefore, was impossible, unless one sat down to supper an hour and a half before sunset, and a half hour later fled to one's tent. This was not practicable, as we had our work to do.

Before leaving New York I had taken the precaution of consulting a specialist about antimalaria injections, and had been advised to wait until I got to London, where there was a hospital for the treatment of tropical diseases. At this London hospital, I was told to wait until I got to Nairobi; that the physicians there knew more about tropical diseases than anybody else. So I inquired at Nairobi, and was advised against injections. They couldn't prevent fever, I was told; quinine alone would protect me. So I laid in a stock, according to the directions of the physicians—one-, five-, ten-, and twenty-grain pills.

One favorite trick of the Tinga-tinga mosquitoes was to alight on your back as you crawled into your tent, so that you unknowingly carried in a dozen or so with you. Then, with a lantern in one hand and a swatter in the other, you began a process of extermination. The enemy, not liking light, sought the walls of your tent near the top, and each time the swatter descended those that escaped would fly about a few moments, and again alight. Some, however, had cunning enough to hide, so it was sometimes necessary, after having gone to bed in fancied security, to light the lantern afresh and go on another hunt. Of course, by this time you knew you had been bitten—you were left in no doubt by sundry burning spots distributed over your anatomy—and all you could hope was to get revenge and pray that the malarial inoculations would not be numerous enough to do any harm. Vain hope!

The people of this country were an offshoot of the Masai. Cattle, sheep, goats, and chickens they had in plenty. One of their villages was within sight of our camp, about a mile and a half away, on a cape of the lava flow.

Everywhere and anywhere you strolled in this region, you were sure to flush large flocks of vulturine guinea fowl, about as big as chickens, which broke cover with a tremendous whirr and fuss. This was what I first encountered when I set out to visit the village. Of course, there were quail in myriads, and I also encountered a porcupine.

W. R. LEIGH.

The vulturine guinea fowl

As I neared the village I saw cattle standing about singly, motionless, listless. I passed close to a big bull, who did not even turn his head to look at me, and when I gave him a slap on his flank he still did not stir. "Curiously phlegmatic!" I muttered.

This village was surrounded not by the usual fence of piled-up thornbushes but by a far more sophisticated fence of stakes, about the size of a man's arm, with the large ends sunk in the ground, and the whole woven together with switches and split saplings. The fence was ten or twelve feet high, very strong, and its gates, closed by bars, were just wide enough for the cattle to squeeze in and out singly. As I approached I found some women gathered around a steer, which was lying on the ground. I thought the animal was dead, and they were skinning it, but when I got nearer I realized that it was alive and was being bled. One woman supported the creature's head, while another held a bucket into which gushed a stream of blood from the bull's neck. They had tapped a vein, and the bucket, a sheet-iron affair obtained from the whites, was half full.

This explained the apathy of the animal I had slapped on the flank: he had been bled half to death.·

I had heard that the warriors of this region, like other Masai tribes, live on a diet of blood and milk: it is supposed to make them brave, strong, and ferocious. As I stood watching this strange performance, a matron, with kindly hospitality, came forward with a bowl of blood and warm milk, mixed half and half, and offered it to me to drink. With the best grace I could I thanked her but declined, although I knew I was honored by being put in the warrior category.

The huts inside the fence were built of straw or grass thatch, conical at the top. A man might stand erect in one. Alongside some of them gourd and squash vines had been planted, and trained up onto the roof, where amid their huge green leaves, enormous salmon-colored squashes and white gourds lay ripening. Just under the eaves of the huts I observed round holes almost large enough to receive a man's arm. When I pointed to one of these, inquiringly, a man said, *"Kwinda la moshi"* (For the smoke to escape).

A woman carrying a long gourd decorated with shells caught my eye, and I offered to buy it. No, it was not for sale. I offered her five shillings. Others clustered around, an animated discussion arose, the owner of the gourd protesting, and other women and men arguing. A man indicated with his fingers the number eight, and said *"Nane!"* (eight). I assented. The woman still protested. I got the words *pega* (strike or beat) and *mume* (husband). She was afraid her husband would beat her if she sold the gourd. They were using Swahili words, although they were not Swahilis. They probably thought I would understand it. At any rate, finally a man grabbed the gourd, handed it to me, and took the eight shillings.

As I looked at the many naked children, I was struck by the fact that nearly half of them suffered from navel-hernia. I suppose some sort of bungling during the birth of the children is to blame. Possibly superstition has something to do with it, as it has with pretty much everything in Africa.

At night the village cattle were brought inside the

pole fence, which of course provided far better protection than any thorn fences could give.

I have called these people Masai, but I am not sure that they were pure-blooded. Their blood-and-milk diet was Masai in origin, but their conical huts and excellent fence were not. Their customs were quite different from the regular Tanganyika Masai, too. Akeley didn't know, either, exactly what they were.

On the way back to camp I followed a path which took me down into the valley where the swampy places lay and where we had seen the zebra herd and the Kavirondo congregation. I found wet spots covered with water grasses, under which was a layer of peat. Here and there were ponds of black water, few more than six inches deep. The ground was spongy, and a whitish deposit around some of the partly evaporated pools suggested alkali or salt. Flanking the wet sections on either side were wide grass-covered stretches of dried gumbo soil, filled everywhere with deep tracks, left over from the rainy season, when the whole place was probably a shallow lake. I judged the water to be seepage under the lava flow from the buffalo swamp.

At this place I met an old native, who came down the trail carrying on his back a wooden *safari-buyu* (carrying bucket). This consists of a board some two feet long, with carrying thongs, attached to one side of which is a bucket about eighteen inches deep. The old man wore nothing but a breechclout and sandals. In one hand he carried a stick.

On coming up with me he halted, grinning affably. If he had had a few more rags on, and had spoken English, he might just as well have been a Negro in my native

State. The instinct for sociability, the good-natured loquacity, and the curiosity to know who and what I was were all so familiar to me! I felt like calling him "Uncle."

I said, *"Jambo!"* (How do you do?), and he replied, *"Jambo, bwana."* (How do you do, Master?) He lowered his burden to the ground, anticipating some minutes' visit. His red gums with sparse snaggleteeth were exposed; his slaty eyes were drawn into slits among his wrinkles. A most infectious jollity radiated from his somewhat odoriferous person. Had I but understood his language he would have told me wonderful stories, no doubt.

But as my Swahili vocabulary was limited, and it was probably not his mother tongue, we were both handicapped. I pointed to his bucket.

"Asali ya nyuki!" (honey) he explained. And lifting the lid he invited me to have some. The fact that there were dead bees, honeycomb, ants and small sticks included in the delicacy was of no consequence, of course, but somehow I did not desire honey just then. I thanked him politely, *"Ahsante sana!"* but refrained. He wanted to see my gun, and when I allowed him to take it in his hands he was delighted.

"Mzuri sana! Mzuri sana!" (Very fine! Very fine!) he kept repeating ecstatically. He looked off to where there were some zebra, and said, *"Boom!"* and laughed joyously. Finally I gave him a shilling, and his delight was genuine and amusing. I said, *"Kwa heri"* (Good-by), and with bow and grin he answered, *"Kwa heri, bwana!"* (Good-by, Master.)

The African native is so anxious to please, and at the same time has so little comprehension of the value of truth, that he is very misleading unless you understand him. If you ask him a question, he does not aim to give you facts, but tries rather to divine what you would like to hear. Thus, if you meet a native on a trail, and ask him if he has seen game, he will say, "Yes, much game"; he knows you are out for game. If you show evidence of believing him, and ask, "Was it big game?" the answer will be, "Yes, very big game!" Then if you suggest elephants, he will glibly tell how he has seen a fine bull with enormous tusks. As a matter of fact, he has probably seen no game at all. Your African is a good storyteller, and embroiders artistically when relating an adventure; he is quick-witted, plausible, and ingenious, but always childish. But it would be a mistake to suppose he is always happy. Ah, how he can suffer! Nothing cast in human shape can express agony more poignantly than the African savage.

The African in America is credited with a marked talent, or aptitude, for music, but in Africa I saw little evidence of this. Our porters had a couple of musical instruments, shaped roughly like a harp or old-fashioned lyre, with a shaft across the top. To this shaft the five strings were fastened, and made taut. The tuning was imperfect, of course, and the resulting falsetto sound had only a remote resemblance to music. To this strumming they chanted an improvised something which bore no relation to the sounds extracted from the instrument. The whole performance impressed me as a crude attempt to imitate something seen and heard among more advanced people, possibly the Arabs. The porters sometimes sang Arab songs, Arabic religious chants, and even English hymns or popular songs like "Home, Sweet Home," all sadly butchered.

Negro music is far nearer to ours in harmony than is the music of our American Indians, but the Indians show a fine originality that the African lacks.

One exception to all this I did note. Kambi, one of our porters, had made himself a musical instrument consisting of a wooden bow like those our Indians use, with a wire for a string, and to this wire he attached a tin can, end on. From this contrivance he got notes by tapping the wire with a little stick, while manipulating it with the fingers of his other hand. His songs were in his own language, and his music had rhythm and well-maintained method. The effect was decidedly pleasing. It was probably derived from music he had heard at a mission school.

Chapter IX

Into the Swamp

MY STUDY OF THE SWAMP was roughed out on the canvas several days before I was able to start painting, because the sky was overcast, and Kenya hidden in clouds.

The volcano, with a five-o'clock evening sun off to the left, was to dominate my background, with a rose-opal sky spread behind it. A few glints of light were reflected from its glacial crest, which rose from a long mass of clouds tinted by the low slanting sun rays. Below the clouds the misty mountain appeared as a lavender tone, and against it the lighter wisps of smoke rose from hundreds of fires among the foothills. Before it lay the broad yellow surface of the swamp. Cloud shadows fell on the foreground, which showed a wall of vegetation, water, and the abrupt edge of the lava flow with its dead grass. A flight of Kavirondo cranes breaks the sky, and above the swamp white herons, as always, indicate the presence of buffalo.

For the buffalo group, as I conceived it, would contain a big bull leading the way up out of the swamp, followed by a numerous herd extending back into the cover. The vegetation should be shown trampled and crushed where the great beasts had wallowed or battled. Yet, I had not seen any such places. The swamp growths where we had camped were undisturbed. The orange-crested plants all stood decorously erect and in militialike order. In among them wound a gentle little open waterway, upon which floated the green, purple, brown, and yellow lotus leaves, and delicate lotus buds and blossoms whose exquisite forms and glowing colors were reflected in the placid water. On this serene flood floated the fallen orange petals of the tall growths; and little light green bits of shore peeped out from among lush grasses that bent over to dip in, and be reflected on, the shimmering tide.

But while the view of the mountain, the wide expanse of swamp, suited my purpose, the foreground would not do at all. When I called Akeley's attention to this—when I described to him my mental picture of what it should be, he at once agreed.

I explained, "There is no evidence that buffalo have ever been within a hundred miles."

"No," he admitted. "We will have to supply that!"

I thought the matter over for several days. I walked alongside the morass for a mile or more, and discovered where the buffalo were accustomed to emerge at night to graze on the lava flow; I found their trail leading into the swamp.

One afternoon I beckoned Ibrahim to follow, and with my rifle walked to the opening of this trail. I stood on the highest part of the lava flow scrutinizing the slough critically. Wherever there is a buffalo herd, there are white herons. Far away—more than a mile—I saw some, but near at hand not a feather. Yet I knew that when the buffalo are lying down, dozing or chewing their cuds, all of the birds might be out of our vision, on the ground.

Again, there are sometimes rogue buffalo, that is, old fellows who have been beaten out of the herd by younger

107

Hartebeest or kongoni

bulls, and who thereafter roam about solitary and morose
and may be encountered anywhere. Yet even a rogue, I
decided, ought to have one or two herons accompanying
him unless—unless he, too, was lying down, and they
were on the ground!

I said to Ibrahim, *"Nina kwenda tinga-tinga ndoni."*
(I am going into the swamp.)

He looked at me hard.

"Tinga-tinga hatori, bwana!" (The swamp is dangerous, Master!)

I took the buffalo trail, walking slowly, my boy close
behind me. From knee-high the vegetation became waist-
high, then shoulder-high. I took a last long look over
the level fields of orange all about me: nothing stirred.
Only a dragonfly flashed by and the chirring of a grasshopper came from somewhere behind. Black mud and
deep buffalo tracks filled with inky water before me, between two walls of green. In a few yards these walls
stood three feet above my head. The tunnel wound cra-
zily, sometimes splitting and coming together again,
sometimes ten feet wide, the next moment scraping my
shoulders. But what I was looking for did not appear.
How far must I go? I looked back at Ibrahim.

"Harufu mbaya!" (I smell a stench!) he whispered.
So did I. There was carrion near!

Still the ebon pools of water and tufts of bunch grass
ahead, and dense ten-foot walls of green on either side.
We stepped gingerly from tuft to tuft of bunch grass;
I held my gun ready, while I realized that I would never
have a chance to use it. We scarcely breathed, so intently
did we listen, as we progressed yard by yard. None of
the pools of water had been disturbed for some hours;

109

three or four yellow butterflies hovered over one. Several large metallic green flies buzzed by. The stench increased.

I said to myself, "This is a damn-fool thing you are doing!"

Just then there was a loud, crashing, whirring noise, and a wild cry. We stood frozen; but it was only swamp fowl screaming, thrashing the vegetation with their wings as they rose almost from under our feet.

I took a deep breath; I could hear my heart.

But having come thus far, I must get what I had come for.

Slipping, splattering filthy water, gliding like thieves, we pushed on. The walls were now twelve feet high, absolutely impossible to pierce, save by laboriously digging a way.

Suddenly we emerged into a large amphitheater, in the center of which lay the carcass of a buffalo cow, dead possibly two weeks. Shreds and slivers of hide and sinew still clung to it. All around were mud, hyena tracks, and loathsome pools from which protruded fleshless ribs, a pelvis, thigh bones, and tail vertebrae with the hair tuft attached. I also saw the telltale feather of a vulture and some flecks of white down. Squawking Kavirondo cranes winged overhead in a long straight line. A pair of black ibis passed. A small bird chirped. A buzz and whine of green flies assailed our ears. The stench was nauseating! It was a horrific scene of savagery and death.

But there on all sides lay the trampled and tormented vegetation I sought. Here the great beasts had wallowed and wantoned; here they had battled and caroused. I studied it all, standing with Ibrahim motionless beside

me. I photographed details on my mind: color—contour
—I had got what I came for.

Another lane opened out of the amphitheater, leading
in a somewhat different direction. Had the buffalo gone
that way?

Silently creeping away—feeling the impulse to run,
but fearful of making a noise, we stole out of the fen;
nor did our nerves cease to tingle until we were back in
the knee-high grass, and away from the gruesome odor
of bog and carcass.

When I got back to camp I told Akeley what I had
done.

He stared at me incredulously. "You're a God-damn
fool!"

It was about this time that Akeley decided to join
the camp in Tanganyika. He and Mrs. Akeley left with
Raddatz; Jansson, Rockwell, and I remained.

Akeley was eager to get the buffalo specimens collected at the swamp, and to see personally that all the
skins were properly treated. He wanted to accumulate
every possible bit of usable material for the African
Hall from this place—yet he took time out to go lion-
spearing! Well, sometimes blessings come like misfor-
tunes. Akeley told me on two different occasions, "I am
going down into Tanganyika to get $500,000 for this
work from Eastman."

It was the first time the suggestion had reached me
that the money for the trip was not all ready, or that
there might be any hitch in getting any part of it. The
whole thing was out of my sphere; I was there to paint.
Nevertheless, I felt anxious for Akeley.

He and I had talked at length about the African Hall

111

while working at the swamp, so I knew he felt it was to be the crowning episode of his life's work. He had made me realize that the main difficulty was not money, but men to carry out the work; men of high grade, with ideals, intelligence, and enthusiasm; men equipped with a rare combination of big qualities. We talked over the artists and taxidermists, the accessory men, and the people who might or might not give the money to get the work done. We discussed the giants that stood in the path of achievement: Ignorance, Folly, Bluff, Commercialism, Jealousy, Blindness—and after these conversations with him I felt that what we were tackling was a new art—the art of habitat-group building; and that very few had the necessary training to do it justice, and still fewer the money, but that Akeley, with proper backing, had the insight, the mental integrity, the knowledge, and power combined with good judgment to do the job.

He told me he expected to return to Africa at least ten times more; that he would complete the African Hall in fifteen years.

In that mood of hopefulness he went off to Tanganyika.

The rest of us were not ready to leave. Jansson and I had not completed our color notes and studies, and Rockwell remained to continue trying for the buffalo bulls at the swamp.

A day or so after Akeley left, Jansson and I moved camp back to the head of the swamp, and presently a large herd of buffalo moved from another part of the morass into our immediate neighborhood. Just where we were, the bog formed a long narrow bay, separated from

the main body of the swamp by a finger of lava a quarter
of a mile long, covered with waist-high grass and some
large trees. In this bay the water was two feet deep, and
the vegetation extremely rank—an ideal place for the
buffalo.

I got up one morning to find real, live, flesh-and-blood
black buffalo within a hundred yards of me. They were
in their safety element, the high weeds and bog; I was
in my safety element, the open plain. They would not
come out after me; I would not go in after them: this
was perfectly understood on both sides. They looked at
me, I looked at them; we were both cautious. As our
darky man at home used to say, "One's feared, an'
t'other dassn't."

Our tents, my sketching umbrella, our movements,
our talk—nothing disturbed the placidity of the beasts.
They luxuriated in their fen, and slam-banged and slash-
slithered about, sometimes visible, sometimes traceable
only by the agitation of the tall, blossom-crowned vegetation.

It was just exactly what I had been hoping to see.
Nobody could ever say now that I did not know what I
was doing in my picture for the Museum.

This same morning I was surprised to discover, on a
gentle hillside rising from the far end of the bay, a rusty,
dilapidated old tin Lizzie of the venerable first Ford
vintage. In it were two Englishmen. They had just arrived, and proved to be friends—a redheaded guide and
his tenderfoot whom we had met at the Waso Nyiro.
They had come to the Tinga-tinga Mcubwa after buffalo, and luckily had found them.

I was curious as to what the redhead would do, because

I could see no way of getting at the beasts, even though they were in sight. I also noticed that only the cows showed themselves; the wily old bulls with the tempting horns had real genius for always keeping out of sight.

The redheaded guide led the way along the peninsula, hiding as best he could in the grass and behind bushes and trees. We all looked on breathlessly. Mwanika was so excited he could not keep still.

"You like to hunt *mbogo,* Mwanika?" I questioned.

"Hapana, bwana! Mbogo mbaya sana!" (No, Master! Buffalo are very dangerous!) But he couldn't help jumping about.

The hunters crept from bush to tree and tree to bush, and peeped and peered while the cunning beasts watched them nervously and shifted from place to place, still only the cows showing. The hunters retraced their steps and came around to our side. The guide deliberated; his hunter stood passively by. The cows looked us over suspiciously and milled about. Mwanika dropped his scouring of cooking vessels and moved about restlessly, as if intent on something. The two hunters started down the edge of the swamp, some fifty steps from it. Mwanika, for some unexplained reason, accompanied them! Twenty yards away the guide halted. Between him and the buffalo herd stood a large patch of the tall orange-crested vegetation, which concealed him from the game.

After a couple of seconds' reflection, he and his hunter crouched, and began approaching the swamp directly, behind the cover of the weeds. And Mwanika was beside the leader! He raced ahead of the leader! He sped to attack the buffalo with bare hands. The freckled, hairy arm of the guide shot out, grabbed the cook by the neck,

114

and hurled him backward. Instantly, like a fox terrier facing a grizzly bear, Mwanika raced ahead on the opposite side of the guide, until he was again in the lead. Once more a bony arm shot out, and Mwanika was sent flying back to the rear. All this went on in absolute silence, and to see what would be the conclusion I waited, eagerly watching. I held my breath. Were we to lose our cook?

But the buffalo must have sensed the scuffling: they stampeded. The two hunters straightened up. Mwanika flew back to his pots and pans. The redheaded guide, with a sardonic curl at the corner of his stubble-fringed mouth, watched the herd recede into the inaccessible fastness of the morass. He turned and, after one disgusted glance at Mwanika, returned to the ramshackle tin Lizzie, followed by his docile hunter.

I had had some experience of such cars—the most soul-trying allies of the hell fiend that ever happened—and I had a sneaking suspicion that because they wanted to get away from there, the infernal thing would refuse to start. But to my amazement, it let out a snort and a cough and hobbled away over the hill in a cloud of dust.

I turned to Mwanika.

"*Mpishi*," I said, "you do like buffalo hunting!"

"*Sipende, bwana! Mbogo mbaya sa-a-a-a-na!*" (No, Master! Buffalo are extremely dangerous!)

Some time in the middle of the ensuing night I awoke from profound slumber and opened my eyes; the light of the moon penetrated dimly through the fly and walls of the tent. I got up and looked out the little window in the back wall, and there, not more than a hundred and fifty yards away, was a great herd of buffalo grazing in

115

the open. The black, shadowy forms in the ghastly light seemed unearthly; enormous, like a troupe of black monsters seen in a dream. As I stood there an old bull raised his head and looked straight in my direction as though he could see my eyes watching him, as though he heard me breathing and my heart thumping. His wide sweeping horns caught a glint from the moon.

I went back to bed, leaving the herd peacefully feeding.

One morning I awakened with pains all over my body.

"What in thunder can this be?" I asked myself. "Have I caught cold?"

I got some breakfast, thinking that would help, and I put my study in position and began to work, or try to—it was not much of a try. I got so stiff and logy that work soon became out of the question. So I put my study back under the cover of the fly of my tent, and went to bed. I could eat no lunch. I slept, but while I slept, I dreamed—dreamed of pains; pains that were getting worse. Rockwell came and looked in at the tent door.

"I've got a terrible cold," I said.

"Or malaria?"

That was a new idea! Yet there was no reason why it should have been, as malaria was the logical thing to anticipate; but I had a fool notion that if I had fever, I would be hot, and I wasn't; I felt chilly.

"Take some quinine," he advised.

I took ten grains; that night I took ten more. I slept better—did not dream. The next morning I got up, but could not eat, and soon lay down again. Between that morning and the next I took forty grains of quinine. I had been wary of it, because I once took a dose recommended by a druggist for a cold; and got poisoned. But the next morning I felt fit and chipper, and put in a full day's work. From that time on I developed no more symptoms.

Rockwell finally decided it was useless to try to secure the buffalo specimens at the Tinga-tinga Mcubwa, so, taking two trucks, he left for a point some twenty miles southeast, on the Thika River. The account he afterwards gave me I will repeat to the best of my memory:

The country to which he went was a rolling acacia-dotted region cut up with dry dongas. It was hard hunting, since there was no safe retreat for the buffalo, like our swamp, and the beasts relied on cunning and speed. Rockwell finally located a good bull (the one now prominent in the buffalo group in the African Hall) and wounded him. Although the animal could still make good speed, he had no thorn thickets to hide in, and shortly before sundown Rockwell finally caught up with him in a dry donga, and ended the chase with a last bullet.

Rockwell had only his gun boy with him, and it was necessary to act quickly, so the boy was sent seven miles back to camp to procure a wagon sheet, skinning knives, and salt, and return with four extra men to help with the skinning, while Rockwell kept guard over the fallen buffalo. Alone, he started a fire, and sat down to wait. A moonless night came on; lions began roaring in every direction, and hyenas yowling. Two lions got the scent of the kill and approached, soon becoming so bold that Rockwell had to frighten them by rifleshots into the air.

117

Hours passed. He began to speculate on the possibility of one of these felines having waylaid his gun boy.

The lions became less and less afraid of the noise of the rifle. Rockwell was afraid to move away from the fire, although fire does not scare wild animals as much as most people suppose. He took to shouting between rifle-shots, and throwing stones. He might scare the lions, but to attack them would have meant a battle to the death, with a grave question as to who would survive. After four hours the boy returned with the needed articles and the help. It was four o'clock in the morning when they were ready to start for camp.

Of course, the cow and calf were easy to get, and the second bull occasioned less trouble, but it took some time, and, as there was little opportunity for washing, Rockwell returned almost the color of a native.

By that time, I had moved back to the site where I had begun my study, and had finished it. I now busied myself painting supplementary studies while Jansson completed the accessory studies of vegetation.

One evening at twilight, shortly after Rockwell's return, we discovered a light at the upper end of the swamp. The light was not stationary, but trembled and wobbled, and gradually increased in size. At times it was obscured for a moment, then reappeared. We climbed onto the roof of a truck to watch it, and when one light became two, we were convinced that we were looking at the headlights of a truck driven by Raddatz, who had come up from Tanganyika to fetch us news and directions; that we would pull up stakes the next day and bid farewell to the Tinga-tinga Mcubwa. And so it proved.

We learned that we had missed a very exciting lion-

118

spearing, in which a large number of natives took part. Both Martin Johnson and Akeley had planned to take moving pictures, and as Johnson was then preparing his film, later exhibited under the title of *Simba,* he was given first choice of positions. But by one of the tricks played so often by fate, the action took place nearer to Akeley: he got the best pictures, and the spearing scenes incorporated in the picture as exhibited were his. Both Akeley and Johnson were working for the Museum.

Chapter X

The Plains

ACCORDING TO AKELEY'S ALTERED PLAN, as conveyed to us by Raddatz, we were to start at once, with two trucks, for the Chapin camp on the floor of the Rift Valley. There Rockwell and Jansson were to remain, assembling specimens and painting studies for a bird group, while Raddatz and I were to continue on down through Tanganyika to Simpson's Camp, near the lower N'Gourmetti River, where Mr. and Mrs. Akeley were camping, and where we were to secure material for the plains group. I was to paint the great expanse of flat country for the background.

The next morning about sunrise, while everybody else was busy getting ready to leave, I found our cook, Mwanika, wandering around amid the grass and bushes, muttering ferocious maledictions.

"What is the matter, *mpishi?*"

"*Fisi!*" Hyenas had carried off two of his cooking pans during the night! The vessels had been left out to cool, and the odor of meat which clung to them had induced the beasts to carry them away. We found them a hundred and fifty yards from camp!

On our way out, we stopped to rest at Kagio, the point where we joined the main road to Nairobi.

All of this part of the country had a layer of oxidized iron ore covering it, and on the roads, this was pulver-

Gnu or wildebeest

W. R. Leigh

ized into fine dust which rose in immense red clouds behind every vehicle. Automobiles, following the lead machine, traveled in a stifling rose-colored fog, and as the occupants of the cars were damp from the heat, they all became incrusted with dirt. To avoid this nuisance the drivers behind the lead hung back to let some of the dust settle, but this did not help much, for the impalpably fine powder hung in the air a long while. Besides, other vehicles than ours were traveling the roads, in both directions. Again, the lead car had the maps, and showed the way, and therefore must be kept in sight, despite the dust fog.

We reached the Chapin camp, eighty miles from Nairobi, at six o'clock one evening.

We made camp there that night, and soon after sunrise the following morning, Raddatz and I said good-by to Rockwell and Jansson, and were off on our trail across the grassy plains.

That same day we halted about noon at Kilima-fetha (Gold Hill). The place is a gold mine directed by an Englishman whose wife and child lived with him in his new stick-and-mud native house. The house obviously had been designed by a white man, but the woven switch-and-clay walls and grass-thatched roof were native. The mine superintendent was an agreeable soul, and his wife a fine type of Englishwoman.

That afternoon we came to a difficult donga. There was scarcely a chance of getting the heavily loaded truck up the far bank at one go. The only remedy was to chuck the wheels. Our natives didn't know how, so I had to do the chucking while Raddatz drove. After some six or eight efforts, the truck made the level. We were streaming with perspiration and covered with dirt. I brought out a pineapple I had bought from some natives a few days before, and cut it in half, as we settled down in the

Waterbuck

shade of a tree to rest. That was the most heavenly pine-apple I ever ate!

Now we began to pass through herds of animals, many of which I had not seen before: topi, eland, gnu, water-buck.

Shortly the small antelope and gazelle swarmed in countless thousands, with eland, kongoni, and topi running together in the same gang. A herd of a thousand zebra insisted upon crossing and recrossing our course, doubling back and crossing again, sometimes as often as four times. The gnu would kick up their heels and perform eccentric capers, often swerving, circling, and cavorting, and engaging in sham battles with each other. The eland would leap into the air and prance, but the impala were the champions. They performed the most prodigious leaps high into the air, apparently for the mere fun of it. The dust they kicked up nearly stifled us.

We arrived at our destination, Simpson's Camp, shortly before sundown.

The next morning after breakfast, Akeley came over to my tent. I never saw a man changed so much in so short a time. He looked ten or fifteen years older than when I had last seen him. His habitual stoop was accentuated, the lines in his face were deeper, his color was gray; he was unsmiling.

"We'll go out," he said, "and look for the place from which to paint the plains group."

We got into a truck and he took the wheel.

The camp was located in one of those flat, scattered acacia forests so characteristic of Africa, but a short drive brought us out upon vast open plains, covered with herds of animals. I had never seen so many animals; it was hard to believe my eyes. Sometimes we had to stop the car to prevent running into compact walls of gnu, kongoni, topi, or zebra. They struggled to get out of the way as quickly as they could, but some could not see the

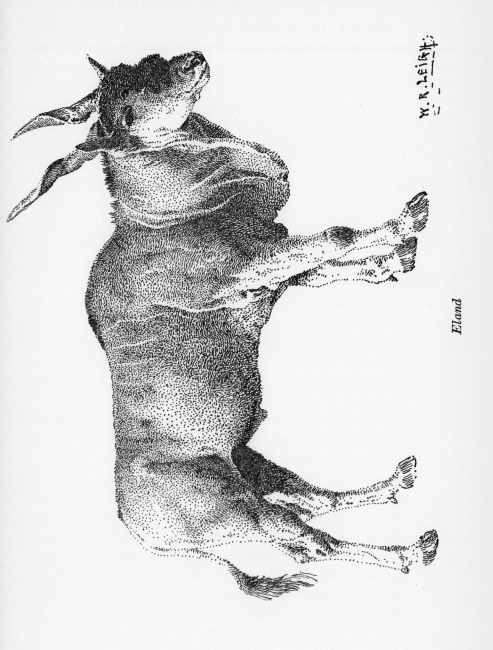

Eland

car because of their fellows, and were slow to take fright, or to be warned, even by the tooting of the horn.

Here, too, the plains had been burnt off about a month before by the natives, as is their habit, and the young crop of grass was feeding millions of animals. Akeley said he thought there were probably five million beasts on these plains, but that on previous trips he had seen about three times as many there.

Wart hog

In addition to the creatures I have enumerated above, there were giraffe, bushbuck, Thomson's and Grant's gazelle, wild pig, ostrich, bustards, secretary birds, guinea fowl, hyenas, serval and civet cat, wild dog, foxes and jackals, and smaller animals. All these we saw commonly, but besides these there were many not so obvious: lion, leopard, cheetah, aardvark, mongooses, baboons, green monkeys, monitor lizards, rock pythons, cobras, and black, brown, and green mambas. In the air there were many more birds. It was marvelous to stand on

126

some hill overlooking these plains, and to see the un-
countable moving creatures receding toward the horizon,
until they became mere series and aggregations of dots,
which grew smaller and fainter until lost in the blue
haze, but never diminished in numbers.

My big study was to show the Tanganyika plains
from the vantage point of such a hillside. At the spot we
chose that day, a tree-lined donga zigzagged from the
middle ground off into the vastness, joined by other
watercourses leading the eye away and away across the
yellow immensity, which gleamed pale gold against the
lilac at the horizon.

Some of the grass had been too green to burn, and
now had shot up and matured so that its ripe seed pods,
seen obliquely from a distance, gave the plains an appearance of light rose-yellow or cream in patches. As
the terrain approached the eye, and one looked down
more directly into the grass, the scattered ripened stems
tended to disappear, and the green became more evident.
In the immediate foreground, where at the time of the
fire the grass must have been very green, and would not
burn, it now appeared matured, abundant, and tawny.

In my picture cloud shadows form vivid bands of
wistaria-purple, and *kopjes* pale into mere shadows in
the distance. On the left a system of hills breaks the
monotony of the horizon. Herds of herbivores ascend
the hillside toward us, or gather in knots about the
trunks of scattered trees, where they are accustomed to
rest in the shade and fight flies.

Watching these myriads of beautiful wild creatures
day after day, the cogitating mind instinctively asked,
"How long can this go on? When will encroaching civi-

lization deprive these animals of their immemorial grazing grounds, break up their seasonal migrations, dislocate their scheme of existence, and sound the death knell

Lion

of the most extraordinary reign of animal life this earth perhaps has ever seen?"

It must be borne in mind that the herbivorous animals, as a rule, must have open plains if they are to exist. Our North American prong-horned antelope are an example.

Masai ostriches, Tanganyika

W. R. LEIGH.

Their defense is speed. If there are too many bushes or rocks under cover of which carnivorous beasts can stalk them, they cannot survive.

Imagine, now, a ranchman putting up a barbed-wire fence across several miles of these Tanganyika plains; then picture lions starting a stampede of a couple of

Lioness

thousand animals in the black night, and these animals rushing pell-mell into the barbed wire! The fence would be demolished, after a number of beasts had been maimed; and the ranchman's crop would be trampled and destroyed. So the ranchman would start poisoning and shooting—and between him and the lions, what would become of the herbivores?

THE PLAINS

Akeley and I drove some five miles to a range of hills, where we stopped and left the car. We had not talked much. It was clear that he was preoccupied, that his thoughts were not pleasant. I refrained from talk because he did. We walked up the side of the hill until we were high enough to command a comprehensive view; then we walked along the range until we hit upon the spot we decided would be the most advantageous for a picture. I took out my handkerchief and tied it to the twig of a tree to mark the place.

There was nothing left then but to return to the car. Nevertheless, we lingered over the scene before us. I said, "This will make a marvelous group—it should be a corner group in the Hall."

"It will be," he returned.

"It will be a page of natural history that will survive, perhaps, after much of this animal life has been wiped out—a record of something which never can be again— a document of inestimable value."

"Exactly!"

We stood in silence again.

"There is no price too high to pay for such a document!" I supplemented.

"Absolutely none!" he agreed.

Another pause.

"Did you get your five hundred thousand dollars?" I asked.

Akeley paused; he looked away across the expanse. I felt his answer before it came.

"The old tightwad didn't give me a cent!" he said deliberately.

W. R. LEIGH.

Chapter XI

Night on the African Plains

W HEN I STUDIED THE PLAINS IN THE SUNLIGHT, with their green-gold carpet of herbage and the countless animals calmly grazing, or when I drove my car out among the beasts, as I did daily, and saw them moving lazily to get out of my way, displaying little or no fear, I felt a warm sense of tranquillity, almost serenity; the wilds were a sea of sunny peace.

But when the sun went down everything changed. Night on the plains was blind but eloquent; its sounds were a revelation!

Night set the carnivores upon the prowl, and put the herbivores upon their guard. There was a tenseness—a sense of brooding suspense in the darkness, a deathlike silence, broken only by the fitful drone of a beetle's wing, the chatter of a bat, the drowsy chirp of a bird overhead, or the somnolent chirp of crickets.

The hyenas, the jackals were silent—tensely expectant; they skulked apart while the prince of killers stalked his prey. The crafty and soft-footed leopard was stealing in and out of rocks and thickets in quest of bushbuck and baboons.

Lying snug in my blankets, with nothing between me and that vast, flat, teeming world but a mosquito net over the door of my tent; looking out at the myriad stars that glittered and twinkled with amazing brilliance in the

133

moonless void; following in thought the Milky Way as it rose majestically from one horizon to arch over the earth and disappear on the other side; blinking as now and then a shooting star drew a line of glistening fire across the spangled sky—I might well have felt a sense of peace, had I not known that in the blind, black night tragedies were enacted such as the day rarely sees; the stillness was crowded with the breathless terror of the hunted, the grim concentration of those that hunt.

Yes, but for these terrors—these butcheries—the antelope world would become so overpopulated that the food supply would fail, and famine would decimate them even more cruelly than the lions. As it is, the less cautious, less fleet, the least fit succumb—the best, or the luckiest, survive. It is the balance, ordained by nature, and obtains among us humans just as surely as it does here on these plains. The streets of New York are a hunting ground quite as much—the struggle for existence is as relentless there as it is here.

Suddenly a harsh, discordant wail breaks the silence of the night. A hyena, half hysterical with pity for himself, informs the world that his belly is empty! Slouching along some near-by game trail, he follows at a distance the movements of the disdainful lion, the scraps of whose feast he feeds upon. In competition with him are other scavengers of the night: jackal, fox, wild dog—even the rancorous and treacherous leopard may intrude. But the hyena is the scurvy and vile thief; he leaps in, after all the hard work has been done by others, and hogs the prize! Surely—surely the lot of the slobbery hyena is a sad one!

A mile away an ostrich booms. Off in another direc-

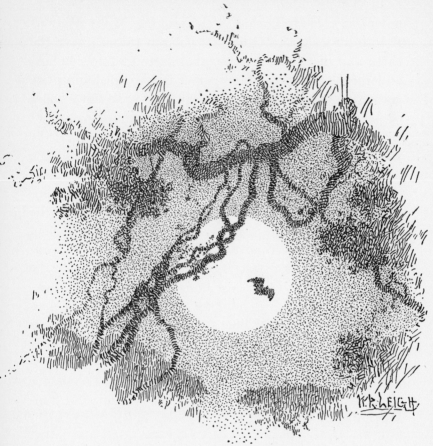

The moon at Waso Nyiro

tion, a zebra barks. And again the owl unburdens his soul. "Go back to your slumbers!" he seems to say.

The moon is coming up. A mellow amber nimbus proclaims its imminence. Slowly, grandly it moves—the orange rim peeps over the margin of the world!

And now it is up—just clear of the hills—the full, round gorgeous moon, salmon-pink—queen of the Afri-

135

Lioness

can night! A writhing vine cuts obliquely across its upper half—a bat flits crookedly athwart its face.

A tree frog's unchanging chant; the scratching claws of a mouse trying to climb the canvas wall of my tent— the many minute, unidentifiable sounds of the night emphasize the silence.

Certainly the owl was right: I am growing tired.

Yet, in fancy, I see the sinuous form of the waiting lioness, crouched, intent. I see the panic-stricken herbivores mill and huddle; they cannot see in the dark as their enemies can. Neither can they think as straight. If they could, they would remain in the open, circling, eluding their clumsier foe, instead of losing their wits in heading for safer regions, crossing the treacherous donga where the lioness—most adroit assassin—lies in ambush.

But listen! What low rumbling begins to rive the air? Like a tempest-driven wave it sweeps toward me! I rise on one arm. What is it? With express-train swiftness it thunders on—it is upon us.

A stampede of wild beasts—a blind, maddened, delirious mob storms right through camp. The ground trembles to the pound of clashing hoofs; pebbles fly, sticks crackle, a billow of dust rolls in at the door.

What in Hades!—has anybody else been aroused? Has any damage been done?

I listen intently: dead silence follows! Not even the tree frog or crickets are in evidence any longer, but from the direction of the nearest tent, something that sounds like a snore, barely reaches the tympanum of my ear.

Still I listen! Minutes pass. The tree frog resumes, timidly; the crickets with spasmodic chirps tune up; the midnight symphony gets haltingly under way once more.

Then, not so far away, from the direction whence the stampede had come, rolls the mighty lion's sonorous war song. The deed of blood is consummated! There in the light of the moon, lioness and cubs stand impatiently waiting until the grim monarch will permit them to join in the ripping and tearing of the limp victim.

The lion pauses—he stands erect—he shakes his scarred and maned shoulders, with one foot on the mangled form before him; he lifts his gory muzzle, as he announces to the world that another proof of his valor quivers beneath his paw.

I drop back to my pillow, and draw the comfortable blankets close around my ears; I have a drowsy picture

Lions in Tanganyika

in my mind of Life and Death stalking each other with infinite subtlety in a universal jungle.

Every morning on the plains Akeley and Raddatz went out to secure specimens—gnu and topi and many others, and there was a constant skinning and salting and skiving of hides going on in camp.

Every morning I and my gun boy drove out in a truck to where the white handkerchief fluttered, and my study for the plains group developed rapidly. The animals, now accustomed to us, flattered us by paying no attention to us—all, that is, but the wild dog. A pack of them came several times to the crest of the hill above, to yelp at me. They are the gangsters of the plains; they never go singly—never attack save in numbers. They are so swift and bold that they will surround even a lion, pile on him, and eat him up. They are greatly feared, for they show little discrimination; a man is just as good grub as anything else.

One day Akeley came across a pack of nine of these wild dogs and bagged the whole lot. It was decidedly a feat to shoot all nine before any could escape.

About two weeks after my arrival at Tanganyika, Akeley failed to rise one morning. He had fever, and was seriously ill. After that day, when I came back from work in the evening, I would usually find him sitting, wrapped in blankets, before the door of his tent. He was always eager to see my study. His great vision, his splendid conception of the African Hall, never dimmed. But something had gone from him. I had only to look at his melancholy eyes, to see it. Of course, I could express no hint of this gloomy foreboding to anyone. Everybody was anxious; no one knew just what was wrong, or just

139

what should be done. But eventually Akeley had to be taken to the hospital in Nairobi. A bed was made in a covered truck, and Akeley was laid on it. Raddatz was to drive. Mrs. Akeley rode in the truck, beside Akeley. A second truck driven by a native, John Willemsen, followed with supplies.

After the Akeleys left, I finished my study and did a number of smaller ones that might or might not come in handily. I wanted to pack my consciousness with intimate knowledge of the many facets of African life, and also to carry back as much painted data as possible with which to refresh and guide my memory.

I took my truck one day and went out to explore some of the *kopjes*. I found them odd islands of tawny granite streaked and splotched by stains and lichens, and rounded by erosion into domes that stood sometimes more than a hundred feet high. They showed forms of endless variety, jutting up from the level bed of the ancient sea that once was here.

They lay in groups; some had dark holes between and under them, and each group was surrounded by a tangled jungle of thorny vegetation of many kinds. Grass fires had burned repeatedly up to the edges of these jungles and there died out. Many of the wild creatures made their daytime homes on these impenetrable fortresses.

Many specimens of gnu, eland, topi, and other beasts were collected at this camp, and an accumulation of meat was the result. After the porters had eaten, and festooned the bushes with quantities of *nyama* (meat) to dry, a great pile still remained which had to be disposed of by the scavengers.

Wild dog

W. R. LEIGH.

One evening, after Radditz got back from Nairobi, he and I drove a truck up to within fifty feet of this pile and focused the headlights on it. Then we turned the lights out, and sat still. In the twilight we saw first of all a fennec fox. He was a charming little fellow, no bigger than a tabby cat, so light-tan that he looked white. His ears were enormous—entirely out of proportion to the rest of him.

Off among the scattered trees were the hyenas. We could see at least twenty pairs of green eyes encircling us, but everything was as still as death. Evidently the frail little fox had more daring than all the big bullies that stood looking on to see what would happen to him, before risking their own cowardly hides. The fennec marched up and got hold of a chunk of meat; we flashed the lights on. But, tiny as he was, the fox stood his ground; he wavered for a moment only. Then he decided he would carry a substantial meal home to the family, at all hazards. The piece of meat he selected was half as big as he was—he could scarcely carry it. But ambition is a great vitalizer. We saw the fox disappear in the gloom, staggering under his load, and immediately a violent wrangle broke loose. It was evident, from the sounds, that a jackal had waylaid the fox, and forced him to give up his booty. The fox reappeared, minus his load, and started to select again, whereupon another rumpus started somewhat farther away. The jackal, in turn, was being relieved of his plunder by hyenas. In a trice he was back, dimly visible, but not venturing to approach the pile of meat—contented to rob the poor fox again, which he did as soon as the latter started away with a second load. The sight of this exasperating waste of opportu-

nity drove the masterminds frantic! The whole plunder-
bund began to chatter and yowl.

We turned the lights off. In a few moments the usual
snapping, snarling, screeching fiends' carnival was in
progress; the hoodlums and racketeers of the animal
world were having their innings. It was a theme and
variations on the hyenas' cacophony I have already described.

The beasts that got to the heap of offal first wanted
to monopolize it, so the only thing the latecomers could
do to make room for themselves was to seize their pred-
ecessors by the hindquarters and drag them clear of the
pile. But no sooner had they jumped into the gaps thus
provided than the expropriated ones took a slavering
death grip on the rear ends of the interlopers. While
pair after pair fell to chewing each other, still others
usurped their places, and buried their heads to the ears;
whereupon the combatants began chewing at the rumps
and hind legs of the most recent arrivals. Thus it became
a question of eating at one end and being eaten at the
other; the buried heads emitted smothered gaspings of
protest, and dragged chunks of meat with them as they
were hauled clear, only to have the chunks snatched
away by new arrivals at the banquet. It was all irre-
sistibly reminiscent of a raid on the stock market.

When our headlights—the light of investigation—were
turned on, all the higher-ups made their getaway except
such as had their heads so deeply buried that they could
neither see nor hear. The blaze of publicity surprised
them, but there was no real danger.

Then the little fellows—crowded out in the melee—
thought their turn had come; they had nothing to fear

from publicity. They jumped in and grabbed a chunk each for the wife and kids at home; but alas! the higher-ups were lying in wait, out in the dark. . . .

The next morning there was not even a blood spot to be seen: the ground had been licked clean.

I saw whole villages of wart-hog holes, all of which had been usurped by hyenas. I imagine two or three hogs dug all the holes. After one had made himself a comfortable retreat, a hyena entered while its rightful owner was away. When the hog returned he found the hyena occupying his burrow, and there was nothing to do but dig another before night, lest a lion come along. But this second hole would be appropriated also by another hyena, and so the poor hog was compelled to dig yet another hole. By the time this had occurred a dozen times or so, the ground would be honeycombed with excavations, all occupied by hyenas. The pig would lose heart at last and seek some other place, and you would find a whole village of hyenas.

Wart hogs do not make their holes just anywhere, but select a high, open spot not likely to be flooded in the wet season, and removed from any dongas, rocks, or other cover where lions are likely to come. Lion, however, hunt out these wart-hog holes, and lie in wait, placing themselves so that they will be exactly above and behind the pig when he emerges. The trick is so neat that it argues extraordinary cunning, or downright thinking capacity on the lion's part. For the lion must know by observation when the pig is accustomed to come out of his hole; he must know that the burrow is really tenanted; he must know the tilt of the hole, and how near he can go and yet not allow the pig to see, hear, or smell

144

him. He must not allow his shadow to fall across the entrance to the tunnel, as that would betray him. Yet when the porker comes to the mouth of his hole to ascertain if the coast is clear, the lion must be in a position to reach down, take his victim by the nape of the neck, and lift him clear. The precision and nicety with which this stunt is executed is amazing.

The lions never treat hyenas as they do the wart hogs. The hyena is so vile that no creature will eat him, not even the other hyenas.

Like a good general, Akeley had given us all our orders before he was taken away. So as soon as our work was done at Simpson's Camp, we started back to Nairobi. Raddatz drove a truck with all the skins and equipment, and I drove a small Chevrolet runabout. I took the lead when we got to the bad donga, but we both made it across without trouble.

John Willemsen joined us in camp one night on our way back, and told us that Akeley would be at least a month recovering from his illness. It might be a mild case of typhoid, but nothing seemed certain, except that we would be in Nairobi longer than we had expected.

When we got there we found that all our plans were changed and our next safari would be into the Belgian Congo, for the gorilla group.

Chapter XII

Gorilla

ON HIS TRIP TO THE KIVU REGION IN 1921, Carl Akeley had secured for the American Museum of Natural History five specimens of the man-ape—three males, a female, and a baby. These, already mounted, were waiting in the Museum in New York for our return with adequate studies and the necessary accessories; not until then could the gorilla habitat group be completed. The animals collected by Akeley had lived on the slopes of Mt. Karisimbi, and our present goal was the spot where the large male was captured.

We remained in Nairobi until October 14, and then started for the Kivu region, traveling in a light car, and followed by motor lorries carrying the supplies and our personal staff. At the suggestion of King Albert of the Belgians, Akeley had invited Dr. Jean M. Derscheid, a Belgian zoologist, to join our party.

The day before we left, I asked Akeley whether he thought he ought to attempt the safari. I did not know what lay before us, but I anticipated a hard trip. He had been over the ground; therefore when he assured me he was quite fit, I could say no more. Some of the doctors, I was told, had called his illness a form of nervous collapse, which is perhaps another name for overwork and anxiety.

We crossed Kenya Colony, and finally reached Ka-

bale, the most westerly British government station in
Uganda, where we left all vehicles behind. From here
we walked to Lake Bunyoni, some seven miles, and then
covered the remaining one hundred and twenty-five miles
of our journey on foot. Two hundred porters carried our
equipment.

Days of tramping over rough mountain country
brought to Akeley's face a worn, weary look that disturbed me greatly. I had not been satisfied by his assur-
ance in Nairobi that he was fit and well, and by the time
we reached Barunga I was still more convinced that he
should never have attempted the arduous journey.

On the second day of our trudge from Lake Bunyoni
our path took us into a bamboo region. Dr. Derscheid
and I were considerably ahead of the party. It was a
wilderness of prehistoric lakes that had now become
bogs: long and narrow, like Norwegian fiords, between
steep, winding ridges, branching out like fingers from a
high central elevation. The lakes were full of black mire,
covered with a heavy green growth of three-foot grass.
From the edges of this swamp, the ridges rose steeply
and were covered with a dense bamboo jungle. Between
the jungle and the morass the narrow road along which
we had to walk had been constructed: it was the only
road. We were carrying our own rifles, having left our
gun boys far behind.

Behungi, the rest station on the top of the elevated
ridge we later ascended, is one of the most beautiful spots
in all Africa. Both going into and leaving the Congo we
reached it shortly before sundown, and saw an indescrib-
ably glorious panorama of billowy mountains and valleys, which rolled away across Uganda in pinnacles and

pyramids, craters, cliffs, deep canyons, valleys, cultivated coves, stretches of level field, shining streams, and
groups of grass huts, all bathed in the magical purple,
rose, lavender, and gold of a marvelous sunset.

Two days more we walked across western Uganda.
We finally reached and crossed the Congo border, and
stopped at Rutchuru, the government station of the eastern Kivu. At Rutchuru we remained four days because
of Akeley's recurring illness. He seemed to have lost his
recuperative power to a startling degree; what was
wrong no one could determine.

Leaving Rutchuru we struck southward toward
Lake Kivu, and a camp at Barunga, on the side of Mt.
Mikeno.

That last day seemed endless. We had traversed rain-
sodden paths through tunnels cut in the heavy vegetation of the jungle. Then came an opening—cultivated
fields, natives with white britches on: we had reached the
settlement of the White Fathers. This Rugari mission
proved to be a cluster of substantial buildings, presided
over by Belgian monks. We passed through well-laid-
out grounds, and were received by the monks very cordi-
ally; they invited us to have lunch with them, which we
did. They were much interested in our expedition. One
of them had ascended Karisimbi and reached the foot of
the final peak of Mikeno. After lunch we went on, and
passed out of the cultivated zone into jungle once more.
A shower passed, and in wet forest and on slippery footing we trudged on and on.

Suddenly, without previous intimation, we emerged
into the light of the afternon sun, just breaking through
the mists, and found ourselves surrounded by grandeur.

GORILLA

We had reached Barunga!

From the spot where we paused we beheld a superb and breath-taking panorama. We were on a shoulder of the twin volcanoes, Mikeno and Karisimbi, but so close under them that foothills and trees cut them off from our view. All about us were the tropical forests of this high valley, six thousand feet above sea level. But looking west the valley lay below us, with here and there pyramidal volcanic vents rising from a floor of dense tropical forest. Beyond rose the awesome triple peak of Chenenagonga against a rose-golden background of sunset sky, a vast purple mass in which could be descried a wilderness of minor peaks enveloped in hazy loveliness. From the summit of Chenenagonga issued an immense column of steam which billowed away toward the north in a long drift. Off to the right of this mountain stood Nyamlagira, less lofty, but belching another titanic column of rolling, undulating sulphurous clouds, their under surfaces tinted a lurid pink from the fiery caldron of the crater.

Between the two volcanoes lay a vast no man's land of impassable lava fields. The sides of Nyamlagira were scarred and streaked with rivers of light-brown contorted slag, their scoriac floods resembling gigantic brown-sugar streams petrified into iron inflexibility.

In the distance, fifty miles away, through a delicate lilac shadow rose the jagged two-thousand-foot cliff of the western escarpment of the Rift Valley, which measures some hundred miles across at this point. We had entered the valley many miles north at Rutchuru, and had reached the center of its floor.

This Gargantuan crack—the Rift Valley—extends

149

through Africa from the mouth of the Zambezi and the Indian Ocean, northwestward, roughly paralleling the Red Sea, up to the Libyan desert, where it ends in a chain of oases. Its length is some four thousand miles, and its course is marked by a succession of lakes and volcanoes. Beginning at the south the lakes are Nyasa, Tanganyika, Kivu, Albert Edward, Victoria Nyanza, Albert, Baringo, Rudolf, Stefanie, Abaya, and Hannington. There are so many volcanoes that I hesitate to list them.

According to the most generally accepted theories of geologists, the Rift Valley is nothing less than another Red Sea or Mediterranean in the process of formation. A hundred million years hence, they think, the eastern part of Africa may be separated from the western, just as the continent of South America is believed to have split away from the continent of Africa, and drifted, upon its viscous interior ocean of molten matter, to its present position. In like manner, the eastern and western parts of Africa may one day drift apart, leaving a new ocean between them.

Barunga is named for a famous old chief, who in 1921 had been very accommodating to *bwana* Akeley, furnishing him with a guide and porters, and giving him hospitable treatment in every way. Barunga was famous as a bandit, however, and had made a practice of killing mail runners carrying letters and small produce between Rutchuru and Lake Kivu. He was dead now, but had left a son—a chip off the old block—whom the Belgian police had chased into the jungles.

On a hill overlooking this site was the village where Akeley had met the old chief Barunga in 1921. As his son, also called Barunga, was unable to be present, his younger brother, whom he had deputized to govern during his absence, greeted us formally.

It is the custom in Africa when distinguished visitors arrive—and all white travelers are highly distinguished —for the news to be sent ahead by means of giant drums. The telegraphy by means of drums has been reduced to a science—accurate information is forwarded.

By some mischance, however, the chief had not received intelligence of our coming, and was unprepared with any ceremony or presents, for which we were rather glad. He was a very nice fellow, and that was more important. An undersized, mild-mannered man, somewhat thickset, he was about thirty-five years old. His pockmarked face was a light-coffee-brown. I thought, as I noted his gentle, kindly expression, that the qualities it showed were exactly those which had determined his aggressive brother to pick him as the relative least likely to develop a treacherous hankering to make his stewardship permanent. It would probably have been better for the tribe if he had been their legitimate chief.

We had arrived at Barunga in the late afternoon and found the usual resthouse accommodations maintained by the government. These were four or five huts of bamboo, cane, and whitewashed mud construction, all looking very neat and clean inside and out. None of us occupied any of them, however. In this wild Africa, there is no way of telling how many natives, between the times when whites visit these stations, have occupied the buildings, or what contagions they may have left behind. We therefore occupied our tents, as usual, and used the doubtful buildings to shelter the loads we had brought, for it had rained during the afternoon, and the trees were still dripping.

Immediately upon our arrival, the chief, anticipating our need for carriers, had summoned his people. Many who had served Akeley on his 1921 trip quickly gathered, including—most fortunately—his former gorilla guide, Mguru, a splendid specimen of young manhood. Mguru's equipment was a loincloth, sandals, a little bit of white down in his kinky hair, and a square-ended sword, or chopper. He was as lithe and nimble as a leopard, and knew the Kivu region thoroughly.

Chapter XIII

The Volcanoes

A T DAWN THE FOLLOWING DAY we set out to climb the volcanoes, Mikeno and Karisimbi. Dr. Derscheid and I took the lead, preceded only by the guide. The sun broke fitfully through the mists, and the beads of rain that still studded the vegetation shimmered with iridescence.

Our path lay between rich crops—beans, sweet potatoes, maize, Kaffir corn, pumpkins, alternating with patches of sugar cane and dense bush, and changed presently to a line of deep mudholes through a tangle of crooked trees. The holes were made by the hoofs of the numerous Indian cattle belonging to the natives, as they went back and forth to water.

By hopping from elevation to elevation between the slime pits, and from root to stone and from stone to root, we reached a sudden rise in the ground, and, passing through a narrow natural gateway between shale rocks, found ourselves at the edge of a circular swamp. This morass was level, and covered with bunch grass two feet high. It was devoid of trees but hemmed in by an encircling wall of dense jungle. The swamp was something over a hundred yards wide, and was evidently a crater. Here the cattle came to drink. In the shale rocks at the entrance were deep holes, slightly larger

153

than a broomstick, and in them lived small birds of very rapid flight.

The guide led the way around the edge of the swamp, where brisk walking alone prevented the spongy black footing from giving way. We reached a stream bed, where the water descended from pocket to pocket in a narrow trough. To follow this road was like ascending a very steep and irregular stairway. Our footing, hard clay or soft rock, was red and slippery, and the going almost straight up and down in many places. Mguru, with two assistants, went ahead to chop a passage up the precipitous slope. Their black backs, streaked with rain and sweat, quivered, muscles bunched and flexed, and naked feet slipped in the mud, but the trail crept ever upward. We progressed by clinging to roots and trees, which showered us with raindrops from their shaken boughs. It was very cold, and every now and then a cloud enveloped us.

Soon we gained a comparatively easy stretch, lighter and more open than the gloomy forest surrounding the crater, and plunged into ten-foot-high grass and bushes matted together by vines. The guide slashed and hacked with his sword, following a trail wholly invisible to us, but evidenced here and there by a cut-off bamboo sapling.

The ascent was still sharply steep in places, but the leisurely pace enforced by this trailmaking prevented it from being arduous. That we were not overweary was largely due, of course, to the novelty of our surroundings; our curiosity was whetted, and our expectation aroused. Every moment wild, strange sights burst upon us; gorgeous flowers—orchids, and many others for

154

which I cannot even suggest names. Bright-colored birds unknown to me flashed overhead; puzzling sounds came from impenetrable thickets.

When we reached the bamboo belt, which surrounds each mountain at a certain altitude, we found evidence of elephant on every hand. They had smashed great avenues through the dense masses of bamboo, breaking the stems like straws, and leaving an awe-inspiring record, suggesting titanic strength and bulk. Our eyes followed these corridors, noting where huge limbs had been torn from trees, where vast feet had left mighty tracks.

During most of the journey we were shut in by dense forest, but occasionally we caught glimpses of the valley behind us. Soon the bamboo became denser and bigger, the trees less numerous. The sun came out, and its light shot long oblique lines of gold dust into the matted gloom, sprinkling the ground with glowing freckles. While observing a bush marvelous in its fancy-ball costume of blossoms, I was struck with the realization that something here was missing! Though the air was redolent of haunting fragrance, there was something wrong. What was it? Suddenly I knew: it was the strange silence—the stillness as of a graveyard. It was the hum of bees I missed—the flash of butterflies. There were no insects anywhere—no flies, no mosquitoes, no spiders. I remembered now that there had been no orchestration of frogs in the crater swamp. I looked in vain for lizards. I was to realize later that we had entered a world where no insect life existed. You could plunge into the walls of luxurious verdure with absolute abandon; nothing would bite or sting. Even the plants had lost their thorns; it seemed an Eden of harmlessness. Yet even as I felt this,

I heard a dull rumble. It was the thud of feet and it reminded me of a stampede of frightened cattle that I once heard in the middle of the night. The guide stood still; we all froze, breathless. After a moment, the experienced savage plowed calmly on into the tangle. Soon we came upon torn-up soil, fresh tracks in the loose black humus. We had stampeded a herd of black buffalo!

Presently we found ourselves traversing a sharp ridge. On the right it dropped ever more precipitously into tangled jungles, with everywhere the alleys and amphitheaters of the elephants and buffalo. Here they had fed, battled, played, and wallowed, smashing and demolishing the verdure with the utter carelessness of prodigality.

On our left the fringe of trees was thin. Overhead the foliage was too dense to see through, but near the ground, where the boughs were less thick, we saw blue distances—not sky, but faraway jungle. We were on the edge of a canyon—a terrific chasm, the bottom of which we could not see, because it dropped perpendicularly, and the edges were so slippery and dangerous that we didn't try. Up from the depths of the canyon mists drifted, no doubt from cataracts, too far below for us to hear them.

Our trail continued to follow the ridge; the sky clouded over; a little rain pattered on the leaves above, but did not reach us. The air was humid but not hot; the aroma of the woods, of the damp earth and the vagrant drifts of flower-perfumed air gave the place a witching charm. Through the bamboo we caught occasional glimpses of the snow-covered crest of Karisimbi. Vistas through the screening leafage revealed lilac patches

156

glimmering—views of the valley we had lately left, seen as from an airplane.

We continued to ascend, and at last the bamboo began to grow smaller and sparser. Our path became a well-defined game trail. Sunlight, returning, flecked and splashed the wilds with vivid blotches and bands of vehement color.

Suddenly we reached the edge of an abrupt drop, and, twenty feet below us to the left, we saw a rocky stream bed. Dr. Derscheid and I climbed down and followed the channel a few yards to where the stream, when swollen, plunged over a precipice eighty-five feet high. Now only a trickle of water flowed over the brink. Below was a tortuous trough of rock—the canyon we had been skirting. The kaleidoscopic change was startling: here at the edge of the precipice I looked off through blue haze, clear across the valley, to gaze with astonishment at the smoking triple craters of Chenenagonga. From Barunga we had seen it foreshortened, and it had appeared much less majestic. Now only fifteen miles away, it was a towering giant, awe-inspiring, sublime, mysterious.

It was midafternoon. We had climbed about four thousand feet and had entered a new, fantastic world.

Only two kinds of trees existed here: the largest known variety of the rose and a kind of mahogany. Our guide stood on the summit of a steep hill above us, in an open spot where one gnarled tree grew. We made our way up to his position. The place we had reached was the small round top of a spur of Mt. Mikeno. It was called Rweru, and served as camp site for parties making this trip. A few rickety and dilapidated bamboo-

and-grass huts were scattered about. Our cook immediately took possession of one, and out of the sodden fuel at hand miraculously conjured a fire.

Rweru was to be our campground for the coming night. The porters with their heavy loads began arriving in rapid succession, and before it seemed possible, the rank grass and wild celery had been chopped out of the way, and our tents were going up. Soon Mr. and Mrs. Akeley arrived with the last of the porters. Akeley looked very, very tired, as he well might. His tent was soon ready for him, and he at once lay down on his cot.

I observed that as soon as the porters had cast down their burdens, they plunged into the dense celery of the little valley, plowing alleys, which forked and branched, but each ended at one of the mahogany trees. These were scattered about as apple trees are distributed in an orchard; they were spraddling, twisted, gnarled trees, festooned with hanging parasitic vines. Not one stood erect; all leaned obliquely in one direction or another. I followed the natives and discovered why they sought the mahogany trees. The thick, leaning trunks of the trees formed ridgepoles over which the extremely long, delicate vines draped themselves, falling in leafy curtains on either side to the ground; their hanging masses sloping outward like the walls of a tent. The under vines had died, and new growths followed, until a matted wall six inches thick was formed between the inner and the verdant outer layers. Because of its slant and thickness, the vine curtain was like a thatched roof, and shed the rain perfectly. Inside of this natural habitation the ground was bare and dry, and formed an excellent sleeping place for one or two natives. These were the "gorilla nests," of which I had been told. There being absolutely no insects or creeping things of any description, these nests were safe and quite comfortable. They admitted neither wind nor rain, no matter how it stormed outside.

The light of the declining sun bathed the mountain in a flood of glorious rose, in which purple and lilac zones of shadow created a wonderful tapestry—a picture of infinite and inexpressible beauty. Now Chenenagonga's three craters loomed splendid and dramatic, while the great crest of Nyamlagira was an exquisite silhouette against the golden West. Its crest of sulphurous smoke turned into a superb pageantry. As I gazed at the twin Titans amid the drifting clouds of mist, I suddenly perceived, beyond, and to the left of Chenenagonga, a sheet of burnished gold.

"Water!" I exclaimed, pointing.

"Yes," answered Akeley from his cot, "that is Lake Kivu."

It was like something seen in a dream.

"Do I see islands?" I asked.

"Yes, there are several islands."

Beyond the lake rose the infinitely delicate silhouette of the far wall of the Rift Valley, and as I watched, the sun sank in a halo of glory, and an exquisite veil of orchid-blue replaced the lake's molten gold.

Suspended from a limb of the tree that stood on our hill we found a bottle containing a note left by the last party that had visited this spot, more than a year previously. "If you want to see gorillas every day in the week," it read, "go up above timber line." None of us understood this message, because the gorillas never go out of the timber. The only tracks Derscheid and I found, when later we ascended Karisimbi, were buffalo and leopard.

Soon after supper the starless night closed in, and we were all glad to get to bed between warm, dry blankets. I dropped into a dreamless sleep, and have no idea what time it was when I was awakened by the strangest hubbub I had ever heard. We seemed surrounded by a legion of demons, yelling and expostulating in a riot of disapproval—of our intrusion, apparently. I tried to guess whether they were birds, bats, or nocturnal monkeys. The cries seemed to indicate good-sized creatures, and they came in waves. Distant voices would be answered by others nearer at hand, and the signals and replies would echo and resound. Presently I noticed that the whole gang of imps seemed to be moving, withdrawing; the whoops and wails became fewer and died away in the distance. It was an uncanny experience, but as no harm came to me or to anybody else, I turned over and went to sleep again.

I learned the next morning that the noise was caused by a multitude of tree hyraxes.

After breakfast Dr. Derscheid began making topographical observations, and Akeley and Bill took the big moving-picture camera and started for the stream. Bill was Akeley's name for the Kikuyu boy, who, at sixteen years of age, had accompanied Akeley on former trips. We had stopped at his hut, after leaving Nairobi, but he was absent. He overtook us in Uganda. We had bright sunshine, and I put in the time exploring the jungles.

Above us elephant grass and celery were eight to ten

feet high, but there was a buffalo trail through them, which led upward, and finally down to the stream half a mile above the waterfall, and up its opposite bank. This was the trail we would follow when we started for the saddle, two thousand feet above us, where our permanent camp would be.

At nightfall it began to rain, and continued all night. Mist obscured the view, and the vegetation being heavily loaded with water, moving about was uninviting.

I was to learn that it could storm here; not boisterously—there was no lightning, no high wind—but meekly, so to speak. A cold, damp draft—a sneaking chill—crept—crept. It merely fluttered the leaves a little and made the celery nod a bit, but it was icy, insidious, numbing. Without any noise or ado a frosty fog would blot out the world; the ghastly contorted trees all about faded into faint shadows—leaving a chilly gray vacancy that shut one in. First rain, then sleet descended, and as the light grew dimmer, we shivered in a dismal lead-gray world of dripping vegetable gargoyles and hobgoblins.

The next day, Akeley awoke with fever and nausea. He said he had had the same symptoms in 1921. The rain continued.

Finally Raddatz and Dr. Derscheid left for the saddle above us, taking the bulk of the impedimenta necessary for our stay there, including some small charcoal stoves and fuel. The higher camp was only two miles from Rweru, but it took the porters, with their loads, three hours to make the climb.

The second morning following their departure, Akeley called me in to him. He had been in bed for three

days, and was still lying on his cot. The door of his tent
was wide open for the air and sunshine. I shall never
forget the look of fatigue and melancholy on his countenance; it touched something deep within me. Although
I realized it was my part to appear cheerful, happy, I'm
afraid there was concern—foreboding—written on my
face.

"You had better take your boys and go on up to the
saddle ahead of me," he said. "We'll follow slowly." He
paused, then looked at me and smiled—a wan, shadowy
smile that came and went, and that left with me a pain
I can still feel.

"I have no misgivings, no apologies to make for the
place, for I know you will find the reality far more wonderful than any word pictures of mine have been. You
will find a place so different from anything you have
ever dreamed of; so fantastic and strange, that you
would not be surprised if you saw gnomes and fairies
among the trees."

Behind the scientist was hidden, unknown to him—
for he always said he disliked verse because it was not
sufficiently direct and literal—the vision of a poet.

I at once notified my boys, and in a few moments my
tent was down, and my belongings and painting kit were
packed ready for transportation.

Mrs. Akeley told me that she and Mr. Akeley would
follow during the afternoon.

Chapter XIV

The Saddle Camp

AFTER WE CROSSED THE CREEK, the ascent was fairly gentle, and the open forest an untouched primeval growth. Mahogany trees predominated. Usually there had been from two to five sprouts, rising from a decayed stump. They were like bearded old men tottering, staggering, clinging together. They made me think of Rip van Winkle and Henry Hudson's crew on the top of the Catskills—all thoroughly inebriated. The rose trees stood straighter—more soberly, more sedately. They seemed to look at the disreputable revelers askance, with puritanical superiority.

Decrepit, deformed, knotted, and twisted, black, brown, lush-green, the mahoganies stretched away in dim vistas—away, away into labyrinthine recesses and awesome obscurity. On every tree grew dark, heavy moss, accumulating—wherever opportunity offered—in enormous bulging knobs and shelves two feet wide, all black and brown beneath, sap-green and velvety on their flat tops. I examined these growths carefully, noting how they built themselves out from the tree trunks or the limbs on which they lay, extending shelfwise. Here and there large pieces of the moss had lost their grip and slipped off, dangling precariously in ragged picturesqueness. Heavy, thick, parasitic vegetation clung to them. Under the shoulders of moss other avid plants had

163

festooned themselves and hung as long-leafed fringes of vivid green, fluttering with every breeze. On the top of the moss platforms dead leaves often accumulated, and in them still other plants had taken root and put forth verdant leaves and exquisite flowers.

Wild celery, torn up by the roots, and smashed and broken for its tender shoots, conjured up vivid pictures of gorillas, for this was their food. They had passed here not many hours before. Nothing could fit into these surroundings more appropriately than those grisly monsters. How perfectly their awkward forms, their ungainly movements, accorded with the grotesque spirit of the place!

It startled me to recall that in all this humid jungle not one animal, not the smallest plant, was quite the same as on the continent from which I had come.

The place was alive with unseen leopards. I saw their multitudinous tracks in the mud of the trail. The leopard feeds on the small bush deer, and the young of the gorillas. It is possible it occasionally kills some of the Pygmies also.

Our three-hour climb brought us to an opening in the woods, and higher up ahead I perceived a wisp of blue smoke; we had reached camp. Soon the grass dining shed, the cook's shack, and the tents that Raddatz had erected came into view.

We were now about twelve thousand feet above sea level, on the backbone of a shoulder connecting Mikeno and Karisimbi, about a thousand feet below timber line. The shoulder, three hundred yards across, was mostly open park. In the middle was a little pond or swamp, a hundred feet wide, irregularly strewn with tufts of bunch grass, and indented with buffalo tracks. This was our water supply.

I stood beside it with a curious feeling. It was unlike any pond that I had ever seen. There were no frogs, no tadpoles, no minnows, skillpots, skaters, sweet bugs; no dragonflies, wasps, butterflies, or mosquitoes—nothing that had movement. It was like some fabled pool of song or story—some unearthly creation of a poet's mind. I could almost fancy Poe standing beside it, murmuring,

It was down by the dark tarn of Auber,
In the ghoul-haunted woodland of Weir.

Silence—profound, oppressive silence prevailed; a melancholy that not even sunshine could dispel pervaded the place. The giant volcanic peaks looked down through the drifting clouds, their stony crests bathed in mystery and awful tranquillity.

Late in the afternoon, Mr. and Mrs. Akeley arrived. Their tents were in readiness; everything possible for their comfort had been done. I had never seen Akeley so haggard—so completely spent. He did not have supper with the rest of us. Mwanika had prepared broth for him.

The sunlight was by this time obscured, and a searching, chilling draft came skulking up out of the wet jungles: it slunk by like a vindictive phantom, snatching with icy fingers at our ankles—the backs of our necks—any vulnerable part. A brisk fire outside the dining tent served to temper the gloom and chill of the oncoming night.

The temperature in this region, while low enough to

numb the fingers, never sinks to the freezing point. Though snow or sleet may fall, and lie for hours in hollows and shaded places, frost never kills any of the vegetation.

That night, between the hyrax serenades, I heard the peculiar grating sound that betrayed the presence of leopards. In this region, where the cats find prey in abundance, there is no danger to man from leopards—at first. But we soon got the uncomfortable feeling that familiarity was breeding contempt.

On the evening of the second day after our arrival, while one of the black boys was coming from the kitchen shed to the dining shed with a tray full of food, a leopard crossed his path, immediately in front of him. The beast did not run, but moved past in leisurely fashion, so close that the boy almost ran into him and was very much frightened. It was already half dark, and it had been raining all day, yet a search for the creature yielded no results, save one or two tracks in the path.

The next day rain kept us in the tents. The fog was thick and visibility restricted. Akeley remained on his cot. Again that evening, as supper was being served, one of the boys found that a leopard was following close behind him. The lad kept his head, but it required courage not to drop his tray and run. Anybody who accuses the African savage of cowardice does not know him.

Our tendency was almost to forget about the leopards —to think of them as a possible danger only by night, if at all. Yet this disconcerting audacity on their part soon jarred us out of our complacency. For instance, it was scarcely reassuring when Mrs. Akeley returned to her tent, after a couple of hours' ramble in the afternoon,

Gorilla in the river

and found a fresh leopard track imprinted over the mark made by her own shoe as she had stepped out of her tent.

On the evening of the second day in the saddle camp, Mrs. Akeley told me that she was convinced her husband was desperately ill. He suffered increasingly from nausea, ate nothing, slept but little. Dr. Derscheid, a graduate physician although he had never practiced, was quite nonplused by Akeley's symptoms.

Mrs. Akeley said her husband wanted me to start without him in the morning and try to locate the point he had kept in mind, and had frequently described to me, from which to make my background for the gorilla group. He had told me that I would recognize it by a bleached old snag, in the crotch of which his big gorilla was standing when it was shot. The smoking volcanoes would be in full view, and below me a great stretch of rolling forest.

He had spoken repeatedly of showing me the place, and I know that he had looked forward to guiding me there and seeing it again himself. He had spoken of it often. Everybody knew this as well as I did, but nobody remarked on it; by common consent we all kept silent, although the same thought filled every mind: Akeley would never see the spot again.

A heavy gloom settled upon the camp. That night still seems to me one of the most dismal I have ever known. The lead-gray fog thickened, the cold wind sighed and rustled the leaves; the rain dripped—dripped —dripped. All night the monotonous drops pattered against my tent; the sneaking wind lifted the fly with an occasional languid flap; the canvas sides bellied in and shivered. All night the hyrax cried like imps or ghouls, laughing, wailing, chattering. All night the grind-grate, grind-grate of the leopard continued. Were the stealthy creatures stalking the elusive hyrax? Were the cries of the hyrax raised in warning?

Once I rose and looked out of my tent flap. The sullen red glare above the crater of Nyamlagira made a gory splash on the black pall of darkness. I saw no moon, no stars, nothing but that blood-red eye that seemed to be keeping watch.

Morning came, finally, with bright, sparkling sunlight. Every leaf and twig trembled with diamond and sapphire drops. And Akeley seemed a little better.

I asked Mguru whether he remembered the spot where Akeley had killed the big gorilla. His Swahili was limited, and mine still more so, but Bill expounded. The guide thought he could find it.

Breakfast over, Dr. Derscheid and I, with the guide, our gunbearers, and Bill, who carried Akeley's elephant gun, set out to climb up the flank of Karisimbi. There was no trail; we had only a general direction to follow. We therefore made our way through heavy vegetation, chiefly wild celery, which stood in a wall shoulder-high. Though densely matted together, it was not especially difficult to penetrate because of the brittle and watery nature of the growths. Some of the bushes bore vicious thorns or nettles that stung like fire and brought the blood oozing from our hands. Frequently we encountered fallen logs several feet through, but so hidden by undergrowth we did not see them until we bumped into them. Upstanding rocks there were none. The whole mountain was composed of decomposing lava, with a surface of soft, spongy black loam, pitted and humped in endless inequalities, which were always gently rounded.

Each mahogany tree was by itself a lesson in personality. Heavy, pink, wistarialike blossoms hung from them all, and the rose trees were covered with golden roses. Soon after we had started, the sky clouded over, and mist again enveloped us. We had brought our lunch along, so we continued climbing. We found an amazing number of fresh buffalo tracks. Many of these places the beasts had recently visited, but the elephants at this season of the year did not come so high up. The thin atmosphere made breathing difficult; my heart pounded like a hammer, and I panted, steaming with perspiration. So did the others.

It did no good to grasp the celery stalks as we climbed; they simply collapsed and gave no support whatever. Each stalk was a tube large enough to accommodate a finger, and its walls were crisp, cool, and soft.

About noon we reached a bench at the upper edge of timber line. It was open ground, dotted with small ponds set in stretches of yellow grass. Here and there were dense masses of shrubbery of new varieties, and low, thick trees resembling junipers, unlike any I had seen below. They were very dark in color and extremely picturesque. A grassy rock-and-brush-strewn slope led from here to the peak of Karisimbi. We were near enough to see that toward the top the grass and brush failed and bare rock vanished under snow.

This open ground was obviously a favorite haunt of the buffalo. Their spoors and the tracks of the ubiquitous leopard covered everything, but there were no signs of gorillas. Enormous blackberry bushes, twelve or fifteen

170

feet high, loaded with large berries, furnished a novel touch and yielded us a good dessert after lunch.

The sky had cleared considerably, but masses of mist obscured what would otherwise have been a magnificent view. We had to use a compass to be sure of the direction in which we were looking.

We finally decided we had come in too straight a line up the mountain, and that in descending we must correct this error, as we had failed to find any view corresponding to Akeley's description.

Had I felt less anxious and uncertain, I would have seized this opportunity to go to the summit of the mountain. But I was so eager to get my study started that I did not take the time. I felt that since the animals for this group were already collected, the whole of this costly expedition hinged upon myself and my studies and sketches. I doubted whether Akeley could recover, and time was precious. It was up to me to find the place and get the studies unaided, save by our guide, whose memory had evidently become hazy.

This feeling of responsibility hurried me back down the slopes, along a different route. But the mountain had become shrouded in mist which constantly grew denser. Soon rain and sleet were falling, and heavy, sullen thunder began to roll. The naked bodies of our boys were streaked with the cold rain and bombarded with hail; their teeth chattered; they cowered, yet not a word of complaint escaped them.

But I did not give up the search. I had figured out in my own mind about where, in relation to Chenenagonga and Nyamlagira, Akeley must have captured the big gorilla. I knew the general location of both peaks, although the mist now made them invisible. At last I came to an open spot; below me lay a dim shadow of treetops; around me the rose and mahogany trees loomed like ghosts. The guide was not sure; but he thought we might be near the spot, and I felt hopeful that we had found it. The sleet came down harder; the faces of the shivering savages wore a pathetic look. It was three o'clock, and getting darker and colder, so I started for camp.

I returned to find depression and gloomy forebodings. Everybody was wet, cold, miserable, silent.

I felt keen regret when I realized I could not tell Akeley I had located the spot he had designated. I was sure I could have seen it from where I had stood, except for the fog, and I thought it would cheer him if I could say I had found it and describe it to him. But I could not see him; he was too sick to be disturbed.

Sleet covered the ground. The fires built by the natives before their gorilla-nest retreats gleamed dismally through the slanting rain. It was another wretched night.

The next morning Raddatz came to me and whispered that Akeley was unmistakably worse. He had been restless and had got up during the night. Raddatz had sat up with him until three o'clock, when Mrs. Akeley relieved him. She was still in her husband's tent. Akeley was lying ominously still when Raddatz left him.

As soon as breakfast was over, I gathered my boys and plunged into the forest again; the air was hazy, but there seemed a prospect of clearing. This was realized, and fitful sunlight dispersed the rags and wisps of vapor. I made for the place I had found the day before, and was delighted, when I reached it, to find it undoubtedly the right spot. There was the grand panorama, the whited snag, the two volcanoes. The guide confirmed my conviction. It was nearing night when I returned to camp. Dr. Derscheid met me; there were tears in his eyes.

"When?" I asked.

"Between three and five o'clock, this afternoon."

"What was the cause?"

He shrugged: "I don't know; something complicated —beyond me!"

I saw Mrs. Akeley for a moment, from a distance. She was weeping.

I knew what I had to do. I called Bill, whose face was streaked with tears. I told him to organize carriers, to get together the paraphernalia I would need for my studies, and to be ready the next morning early to go to prepare my new camp site, some five hundred feet higher on the mountainside.

That was November 17, 1926. We took turns sitting up throughout the night with the body. My watch lasted from midnight to half-past five. The rain had ceased temporarily; the moon was brilliant; the snow-clad top of Karisimbi shone like burnished silver against the black sky where glittered a myriad of stars. The cries of the hyrax and the leopard never ceased. It was very cold, so cold that my blanket and two charcoal burners barely kept me from a chill. Heavy drops of water from the rain-soaked trees kept pelting the tent fly over my head in irregular but monotonous patter. From Mrs. Akeley's tent I heard occasionally the mutterings of

173

troubled sleep. I knew Dr. Derscheid had given her a sedative.

It was a dreary experience, sitting in the dead of night on this lonely mountain amid primeval savagery, and thinking of the career cut short; realizing that a great man lay dead here. For Akeley was a great man—an idealist in the highest sense. He had given his life to pursuing a magnificent idea; he had died a soldier on the battlefield of science.

Chapter XV

Alone in the Jungle

I WAS ANXIOUS to start my study as soon as possible, but a considerable amount of work had to be done on the saddle. The ground needed to be leveled off and tents had to be set up. My large work tent, or fly, had an open end facing the scene I was to paint. At its opposite end, on a terrace two feet higher, my sleeping tent was placed.

Around the edges of both tent and fly, I had gutters dug, and everything made extra fast with lines, for my position was an exposed one. The open end of my fly looked over the brink of a steep declivity. First came a drop of several hundred feet overlooking a great forest, which retreated wave upon wave to where the trees ended, and then the eye sank to the valley, six thousand five hundred feet below. The two smoking volcanoes and Lake Kivu made a dramatic motif.

On the right lay the slopes of Mikeno, on the left those of Karisimbi. It was an ideal setting for the gorilla group. The old bleached snag was one of the chief landmarks by which I was able to identify the spot which Akeley had had in mind. He wrote, in *Brightest Africa:* "As he [the big male gorilla in the African Hall group] reached the top of this ridge he came into full view perhaps fifty yards from where we were. Bradley fired again. This shot sent him rolling down the slope,

175

stone dead. He lodged against the base of an old tree. He was a . . . huge creature weighing three hundred and sixty pounds."

The tree referred to was a dead mahogany, bleached silvery white and covered with gray moss that swayed in the wind. It also bore many clumps of green moss. We brought portions of it back with us, and a part of it appears painted behind the hill upon which our old-man gorilla is standing.

It was unusual to find an old bleached snag like this, alone in an opening. But fires create such openings from time to time, and their tracks may be traced in the green-and-brown pattern that I have painted on the slopes of Mikeno, in the gorilla group background.

By nightfall I had everything ready to begin work, and I returned to the main camp. Raddatz was digging in the rotted lava bed; some of the boys were helping him. All the tools they had were a spade, two axes, and a dull handsaw. He took me to his workshed, and in a shut-off compartment showed me all that remained of our leader. Akeley's face looked so calm and peaceful it was difficult to believe he would never speak to us again. I found Derscheid in his tent. His head drooped; he wept as if he had lost a brother.

Mrs. Akeley remained in her tent.

A runner had been dispatched down the mountain with a cablegram to the Museum in New York City.

I stopped to speak to Bill. He wept as he told in halting words the story of how, long before, he had saved Akeley's life by shooting an elephant that would otherwise have killed him.

He said that *bwana* Akeley and he, following a herd

176

of elephant in the jungle, suddenly found themselves within twenty feet of a big bull elephant. They were directly behind the beast—it had not seen or heard them. To move at all was perilous; both stood still, Bill, with an extra gun, some three feet behind Akeley.

While Akeley's attention was fixed upon the motionless bull, Bill discovered a cow elephant charging directly at Akeley from a different quarter. Akeley did not hear or see the cow. To speak under such circumstances was extremely dangerous—seconds were hours. . . . Bill fired. The cow turned aside. Akeley was so intent that he did not know what had happened, and threw his hand backward, slapping Bill across the face, for a supposed infraction of orders. Bill knew he had saved Akeley's life, but Akeley, he believed, never to his dying day realized why Bill had disobeyed orders.

Bill told me because I was Akeley's friend, and a white man. It had grieved Bill sorely at the time it happened, and now, in his grief, he repeated his version of the story, so that I could get it straight. Then I, a white man, could tell the truth to the world. It mattered a lot to Bill.

As a matter of fact, Akeley gives an account of the adventure in one of his books, and there seems no doubt that he did, finally, appreciate Bill's intention. He tried later to make Bill realize that the misunderstanding no longer existed, but it is difficult to know what a native understands or how he interprets it.

Raddatz had dispatched a gang of boys down to a sawmill between Rutchuru and Barunga for mahogany planking, and others to Kabale, one hundred and twenty-five miles away, for cement with which to make

177

a covering slab for the grave. As there was nothing I could do, I hurried back to my camp the next morning, and set to work. I was fortunate in having a clear day, and got well started before the weather changed. It was cold—so cold that I sat with a charcoal stove between my knees, and my paints became so stiff that they were hard to manipulate. The wind kept tugging at the fly, and at my canvas, making it teeter and wobble, until I had to sit with my palette on my knees, holding the canvas still with one hand and painting with the other.

Fog made the afternoon of the third day quite useless, so I remained at the main camp. A grave eight feet deep had been dug, and lined with new planks. There was a sense of stupefaction over the whole camp, as if everybody had been shocked into silence. All the merry laughter from the cookshed ceased; the gangs of natives distributed among the forest trees went about their work as if their tongues had been paralyzed.

We buried Akeley on November 21.

After that I moved to my own camp, and stayed there until my work was done.

Chapter XVI

Monster Apes and Midget Men

FOOD WAS RATHER A PROBLEM, just then, in the lower camp as well as in mine. The White Fathers had promised to send adequate supplies of fresh fruit and vegetables; but somehow food was scarce. Every drop of water from our lake not only had to be boiled, but alum had to be added to precipitate the sediment. We had chickens and plenty of eggs, and Mwanika made delicious fresh bread every day. We had to have an occasional steer and some goats brought up to the main camp as food for our boys.

Almost every day I could hear leopard in the forest below me; every night I heard them around my tent; every morning their tracks were in front of my door.

The gorillas, however, kept silent except when they fought. I frequently heard their family rows—sometimes below me, sometimes above, sometimes almost alongside. An obstreperous brat would be the cause, apparently, for first the squeals of a cuffed youngster would break the silence; Mamma would remonstrate; Papa would lay down some weighty observations; then a temporary calm would follow.

Fantastically ugly, when first sighted in his native haunts the gorilla gives the impression of unreality; of being some monstrous apparition conjured up by the imagination, wildly and appallingly hideous.

179

Black, ungainly, with small, cavernous eyes of red under beetling brows, he has huge, flat, flaring nostrils, and his repulsive muzzle is surrounded with ragged whiskers jutting from huge jowls. With his vast mouth open disclosing his fangs, he appears to be anything but an animal—a devil of the forest; a specter; a terrific nightmare phantom.

It is impossible to have in his presence the same sensations as when facing a lion, an elephant, any other member of the animal kingdom. It is impossible to escape a creepy suspicion that here is a creation higher than the brutes; a survival, by some mad trick of nature, from the dim dawn of history—somewhere back beyond the glacial age. He seems a Neanderthal man—a remote kinsman, whom you instinctively hesitate to slay because it would seem too much like murder.

The man-ape arouses in you a psychological reaction no other animal produces. You know he is not a man, yet you feel that he is not a beast in the same sense that other animals are. Strange fancies race through your brain. Is this what we all looked like a million years ago? Do creatures like this rule on the moon or on Mars, supreme in some far-off sphere, as we on earth? Those irresistible feelings of fascinated terror, as you gaze at him, arise from no conscious train of thought: they are purely emotional, but none the less gripping, inescapable, and spring from the humanistic actions and attributes of the gorilla, as well as from his appearance. For not only does he look like a gnomish man—he acts like one.

When enraged, this great ape rises to an upright position and clubs his chest with his fists, as a man strikes his chest when boasting of his own strength. He brandishes

these fists as no other creature does except man. He
stands at a man's height, five feet five to ten or eleven
inches; he weighs from two to three hundred pounds.
He utters a roar of wrath which has a haunting resemblance to the bellow of drunken dock hands whom I have
seen fighting on the New York river front. He does not
seize you first with his teeth, but grips you with his
hands. No other creature but man fights this way.

When the first Carthaginian, Roman, and then Portuguese explorers saw and described the gorilla, he entered the realm of the fabulous, and although many centuries have passed, and he has definitely emerged from
mystery, he is still imperfectly known. Has he the rudi-
ments of a language? Does he use any implement? How
fast is he evolving? What will he become?

He has been pictured and romanced about until he
has become a sort of hobgoblin, a bogy: all sorts of un-
true tales of him are current. But see him—see him amid
his haunts in the jungle, and all silly fictions fade and
he stands before you, an appalling reality.

Staring at him for the first time amid his own wild
jungles, I was dazed. I had to clear away the cobwebs
of legend and tradition from the attic corners of my
brain, rub both eyes, and look again—and again! And
yet this lumbering thing, which seemed to me a neg-
lected—unfinished—piece of nature's handicraft, was in
his own surroundings more fit than I. He was kin to the
pygmy, with whom he dwelt peacefully on these forest
heights, and the gorilla's vocal eruptions sounded about
as human to me as the jabberings of the dwarfs.

In spite of the gorilla's silence, I could never forget
their proximity. I felt that, like the leopards, they were

181

forever watching me, but with very different eyes. The gorilla's eyes are small, ugly, red, yet not terrible—not the wide, yellow glassy globes of the murderer. The smooth, lithe, beautiful leopard is far more dangerous, for he is subtle and treacherous, whereas the gorilla, though uncouth and monstrous, is forthright. There is no question but that the gorillas saw me; no doubt they came every day to look at me, but they rarely allowed themselves to be seen.

I knew all the time that I was being studied—that every movement I made was being observed. Yet I had no fear. I made short excursions into the forests around my tent for the sake of exercise, and I always kept a sharp lookout for any kind of wild life.

Some say that the gorilla will never attack a man, even under provocation. Others declare that though he will rush at you with a great show of ferocity, he will never charge home. He has even been called timid. While I believe he is not so much to be feared as his appearance would suggest, I see no reason to suppose that such a creature is timid. Makusudi, our headman, an intelligent and convincing person, assured me the gorilla is a formidable foe.

He told me that when he was a stripling he had been gunbearer to an English hunter on the west coast of Africa. In a hilly but low region on the west coast, the same gorilla occurs as in the Kivu, minus the heavy suit of hair of the mountain gorilla. Makusudi said his Englishman wounded a male gorilla; the animal charged. It ran on all fours until it came close, when it rose on its hind legs and grasped the Englishman with its hands. It drew the victim toward it, seized and held him with its

A gorilla hunt

teeth, then thrust the man's body away, and so, dragging and pushing, it tore the hunter limb from limb.

Many will retort: "The native African cannot be believed." Nevertheless, I think it safe to say that the gorilla's ferocity is still an open question.

I believe he is a very dangerous beast. I argue this from his build and physical equipment. Why was he endowed with such teeth and such strength, if not to use them?

Nature has armed the man-ape, and when I consider the fact that if he could not cope with the leopard he would have become extinct long ago, I hesitate to brand Makusudi as a liar. I think it very misleading to say the anthropoid ape is harmless. To conquer the leopard singly and barehanded, the gorilla must be a gladiator of no mean capacity.

The gorilla's chief and almost only foe is the leopard, which skulks behind, or on the skirts of the bands of apes, continuously seeking opportunities to seize a baby. I was told, however, that a leopard will never tackle an adult gorilla if it can be avoided.

The statement has been made that these apes are not arboreal; that they never ascend trees. Again it is averred that only the young climb to any height. Both assertions were flatly contradicted in my presence, while I was in Africa, by several reputed eyewitnesses. Indeed, gorillas have been photographed high up in trees, and Martin Johnson assured me he had seen the adults climb the very tallest.

It is a singular fact that the Congo Pygmies inhabit the same regions in the Kivu as the gorilla.

Dr. Derscheid told me that while he was exploring

the volcanoes one day, he blundered into a Pygmy village. Their abodes were so irregularly placed, and so overgrown with creepers, that he was in the midst of them before he knew it. They had built low shelters, like gorilla nests, and no discoverable trail led to them.

Before the advent of the white man the Pygmies relied solely on robbery for all their implements of peace or war, and habitually stole from the agricultural peoples in the valleys. Being past masters in the art of hiding and stalking, they hovered around the borders of the fields, watching for opportunities to steal a hoe, a pot, a chopper—anything they take fancy to or find useful, including food. For they make nothing, cultivate nothing.

Now, however, elephant ivory constitutes their chief source of revenue, and they trade it with the whites for whatever they need. I have heard that the Pygmies kill more elephant per year than all the other people in Africa combined. They are said to be the elephant's worst enemies. They use various methods in hunting the pachyderms. One, which a native described to me, is as follows:

Three of the tiny men start together; they are naked, and armed with spears, swords, or blunt-ended choppers, ground very sharp. They advance, perhaps twenty feet apart, all abreast, moving slowly, silently, breaking no vegetation, merely bending it sufficiently to permit their passage. As soon as they approach a herd of elephant, whose proximity is easily known by the noise of breaking trees and the rumble of digestive organs, the hunters smear themselves with fresh elephant dung. This renders them safe from detection through smell. The hunters are so small and so adroit that they travel all through,

African elephants

or around the scattered herd, and pick out the one with the largest tusks. Then two of them conceal themselves, one on either side of the selected victim, while the third places himself in front. At a signal, the man in front shows himself, draws the elephant's attack, and, as the animal charges, the two men on the sides close in behind and hamstring the quarry with their swords. The helpless elephant is then speared to death.

A second method is to excavate a pitfall in the elephant's path, and when one falls into the trap, to spear it. But this method is not popular: it entails a great deal of labor, and often a cow or calf elephant, useful only as food, falls in.

A third method, more to the taste of the Pygmies, yields better results and involves a very dramatic procedure. A hunter, armed with a sword, stations himself on the limb of a tree overhanging some elephant trail. He is hunched up, and screened by leaves to resemble a lump of moss. Several companions with swords and spears hide among the bushes on the ground. They have to wait a long time, perhaps, but sooner or later the game comes their way. As the animals pass under the tree, the man in the branches selects a big tusker and drops astride its neck. Of course, the first thing the beast does is to throw up its trunk, and this the hunter promptly cuts off with one stroke of his blade. If he succeeds only in clipping off a small portion of the trunk, the animal will probably try again, only to lose another section of its main weapon. The remainder of the herd stampedes while the hunters concealed in the vegetation dart out to kill the disabled elephant with their spears.

A fourth method is to shoot poisoned arrows, but after

an elephant has been wounded in this way it has to be
trailed until the lethal poison does its work. This method
sometimes takes several days, and the ivory, the chief
object of the chase, often has to be carried back long distances. In these encounters harm seldom comes to the
hunters; they are too agile and experienced.

I have never heard that Pygmies and gorillas interfere with each other. Neither has anything the other
wants.

The gorilla is herbivorous here in the Kivu country
because other food is not available; yet I fancy he would
eat grubs, grasshoppers, or birds' eggs if he could get
any. He has no fixed abode, but travels constantly, halting for the night wherever darkness overtakes him.

The mountain gorilla never descends below eight-
thousand-feet elevation; he thus escapes diseases which
in captivity soon prove fatal. He also escapes the depre-
dations of the valley natives, who avoid the cold of his
domain. Unmolested, his normal span of life is probably
about the same as that of a man.

When I made my next journey down to the main
camp, Akeley's name was indented in the wet concrete
of a slab laid on his grave.

The boys sent to fetch the cement had taken eight
days on the trip, and then brought only a small part of
the barrel of cement, much being lost or perhaps thrown
away, as it was very heavy. Raddatz sent them back for
more, to be brought in burlap bags; two boys to carry
each sack, with twenty-five pounds of cement, one running with it until tired, then passing it to the other. Raddatz offered them a dollar for every day saved on the

second attempt. They went over the mountain by a short route, and made the trip successfully in three days.

An avenue of little trees had been planted leading to the grave. A cablegram from the Museum had assigned Mrs. Akeley to head the expedition. Raddatz was soberly busy making plaster casts of leaves and flowers.

Chapter XVII

Farewell to the Congo

A T MY CAMP ALL WENT WELL, but slowly. Often clouds would obscure the view for a whole day at a time. I had to be unremittingly alert, ready to work a few moments whenever possible.

Every evening I had to take my canvas well back under the fly, lest rain drench it during the night. Many a time the rain pattered drearily all night, and the trickle of water in the gutters made a doleful sound.

I read myself to sleep each night by the light of my tent lantern; often I lay awake for hours. When I did sleep, it was under three or four blankets.

One day while I was busy painting, I heard an uproar in the forest above, followed by a shot. I wondered what was going on, as it seemed only a short distance away. But the light was good, and the moments precious and so I did not stop work to investigate. Twenty minutes later, Dr. Derscheid came into camp and announced that he had been charged by a gorilla. He had been following a band of the simians, hoping to get photographs, and his confidence had been increased by the experience of several days. Only the previous day he had followed another band for an hour, getting within thirty yards of the last members, which were always old males, keeping the rear guard. But because of the poor light and the distance, he had failed to get pictures, and the following

190

day, with sunlight in his favor, he was bent upon utilizing opportunity. He had reached the crest of a hill, looking across a sharp dip which separated him from another rise. On the far hill, seventy-five yards away, a herd of eight or ten females with babies were retreating. There were three males. He was trying to get them in the field of his camera when abruptly, out of the vegetation in the bottom of the dip, less than thirty yards from him, other gorillas appeared, and a huge male charged with an angry roar. Derscheid stood his ground, but his gun-bearer, who had been ten feet ahead of him, sprang back and stood with poised spear. The doctor, fortunately, was carrying his gun. Akeley, in one of his books, calls the gorilla a slow beast, but this one, Derscheid said, came too fast for any man to have escaped by running, even if the heavy vegetation had not made flight impossible. The beast's mouth was open, his jaws moving from side to side, his fangs gleaming, everything about him in motion except his terrible eyes, fixed on Derscheid. Hoping the gorilla would halt, Derscheid held his fire, but the beast, emitting a terrifying succession of roars, came straight on. Derscheid described the creature's motion as an incredibly rapid, waddling run. When it was within eight feet of him, it rose, ready for action, and Derscheid fired. The gorilla staggered, wheeled, and made off.

I accompanied the doctor back to the spot where the incident had occurred, for he had no license to shoot a gorilla, and he wanted me as a witness to the fact that he had fired in self-defense.

The somewhat trampled spot where Derscheid had stood was marked by a brass cartridge ejected from his gun, and a little blood and a bit of hair from the gorilla showed where the latter had stood. The distance between measured exactly eight and a half feet.

We spent several hours following the trails of the animals to ascertain whether or not the creature had been seriously injured, but we could find no trace of him, not even a spot of blood; so we decided the wound was probably not a fatal one. Derscheid was disturbed; he hated the idea of a slowly dying animal dragging on through several days. He asked me what I thought. I assured him he had acted only as he was obliged to, and should dismiss all self-criticism from his mind.

The next day Derscheid told me he was going to make an effort to reach the summit of Mikeno. Consequently I understood, when, the following evening, I espied a light high on the side of the mountain. He related his experiences to me afterwards.

Upon establishing camp on the evening in question, upon the crest of the pyramidlike lower peak of Mikeno, he found that a deep canyon lay between him and the main peak. In this ravine fine water was in plain sight, cascading down over the rocks; but when he ordered some of his natives to descend and fill a couple of buckets, they rebelled. There were devils in the canyon! It meant death to descend to the water. They preferred to descend the full height of the peak, to the saddle, and bring water from the pond!

The following day Derscheid and Bill made a try for the top. The ascent was very steep, and dangerous, because all the rocks were coated with water-soaked moss, which had no firm hold on the surface beneath. Any patch of moss under your foot was likely to break from its mooring without warning. The wet black ooze underneath acted like soft soap, while the upper surface of the moss clung to your shoe—a perfect toboggan! To scale the final rock splinter on the summit, between eighty and a hundred feet, called for ropes. Since these were lacking, the attempt had to be abandoned.

One evening, seeing Mikeno marvelously lit up by the setting sun, I thought of the sight as symbolical. At the foot of this peak lay our revered leader. Fortunately, I had an extra canvas with me. I grabbed it and secured an impression of the peak before the light failed me. Several days elapsed before there was another favorable sunset effect, but upon this second occasion, I finished the study, which is now in the American Museum of Natural History, where it may be seen by any one interested. When Derscheid saw my large study finished, he remarked it would delight His Majesty the King to have a replica of the study. I said I would keep that in mind. Shortly after this, Mrs. Akeley came up to visit me, and was delighted with what I had done.

I told her of the doctor's observation concerning the King of Belgium and my answer. We at once decided that as soon as I got back to Nairobi, where Raddatz could prepare me a fitting canvas, I would execute a replica for His Majesty.

It took me some two weeks to complete the main studies at my gorilla camp. When I had almost finished these, Raddatz came up, and attached little pieces of white cloth to certain plants which were to appear as foreground detail in the group, and of each one I made an intimate study in color. Raddatz would make his plaster casts of the same plants, and each would be aware of

193

what the other was doing, although we worked in separate camps.

When I finally returned to the main camp, my work finished, on December 11, Mrs. Akeley suggested that I go at once down into the valley, to the lava plain south of Barunga, and from there make a study looking back at the twin peaks of Mikeno and Karisimbi. So I had Bill prepare for my starting the next morning.

Although my gun boy accompanied me, I carried my rifle myself on the way down the mountain. Fortunately I had no occasion to use it. Several times suspicious sounds halted us, but nothing developed.

The weather was fine and the going good, although a little boggy in spots.

At the Barunga camp ground I halted for the night. A band of porters carrying accessories in the form of logs and branches of trees, leaves, rocks and parcels came down in our wake.

These boys—who are not really boys, but men—are all assigned to the work they do by their chief, and are held strictly accountable. This explains largely, of course, why they are so reliable. The poor devils will undergo almost anything.

Their chief was brought to me in the morning, and with the help of our head-man, who spoke fair English and good Swahili, I was able to negotiate with him. He was the undersized, deputy chief with the pock-pitted face. He had eight wives, and I don't know how many children.

The pock-marked gentleman was most friendly, and invited me to pick out any point I found most suitable to my purposes within his domain. The territory governed by one of these chiefs is usually not more than ten to twenty miles square.

When all my porters were ready I set out, in company with the chief and my gun boy, to find a spot which commanded a good view of the two mountains. Leaving Barunga we traveled toward Lake Kivu about a mile and a half. Here I called a halt, for we were in the right position, and needed only an elevation to lift us above the obstructing forests. We turned at left angles, and proceeded between fields and gardens to the village of the chief. It consisted of the usual cane and mud huts, with a few granaries raised five feet upon stilts. Near this village a conical hill rose to a height of more than a hundred feet. I climbed it and found it ideal for my purposes.

After the ground had been cleared of vines, bushes and rubble I had my working fly and tent set up and by afternoon I was at work.

Here, as elsewhere, I and my painting had about the same effect as Barnum's circus on a rural settlement in the Far West. Every day the chief, among others, came to see what I was doing, and approved with a genial grin. He then made himself comfortable beside the cook's fire, and conversed affably with all hands. We addressed him as *Sultane*. Mwanika, canny and diplomatic, was expert in discouraging other loafers, but His Majesty was an exception. The tactful cook always invited him to sample bits—substantial bits—of the viands as they were prepared. A cup of coffee (*kahawa*) with sugar (*sukari*) and cream (*siagi*). Slivers of meat (*nyama*) with salt (*chumvi*) on it, and pepper (*pili-pili*). Bread and butter, crackers, pickles, sardines, were

195

all appreciated by His Highness, as were cigarettes. Milk chocolate was a delectable treasure which was made to last as long as possible. The conversation was jovial, and the chief approved of us heartily—one and all. He beamed upon us, especially when he held a cup of coffee in one hand, and a sandwich of bread and corned beef in the other.

The company was enlivened by the arrival on occasion of Tumbo (Belly) our runner between Rutchuru and the main camp. My camp became a convenient half-way station for him. He was not slender like the traditional runner, but rather stout, with noticeable girth around the waist. He boasted that he could eat forty pounds of meat at a sitting. Allowing for enthusiasm, a dramatic sense, and pardonable misconceptions regarding weights, it was conceivable that he could handle two pounds. This man of about thirty had traveled from Rutchuru clear to our main camp in a day, more than once. He had a big mouth and laughed easily.

I had almost completed my study of the mountains, and was calmly working away one bright afternoon, when I was startled by some fifteen or eighteen shots fired in rapid succession. The sound came from the direction of the left-hand flank of Chenenagonga, among the foothills. A light wind was coming in my direction, and I judged the sound must have traveled about three or four miles.

The next day, Dr. Derscheid dropped in on me, and I got the explanation. The shots I had heard had been fired by Belgian police, out to capture the forceful brother of the deputy chief. They had killed a couple of his followers, but the wily Robin Hood of the African jungles had escaped again. They had been hunting him for several years.

Dr. Derscheid had ascended Nyamlagira, and his description made me long, more than ever, for an opportunity to do some exploring myself. He had found the lava fields passable only in a few places where the hoofs of buffalo and the weight of elephants had reduced the knife-edges of the lava to something which shoes could withstand. These are the lava flows shown in the Gorilla group, descending the slopes of Nyamlagira.

Mrs. Akeley arrived at camp just as I finished my study, and was greatly pleased. December was now in its fourth week—and the next day, the twenty-third of December, we began our journey back to Rutchuru. Shortly after we arrived, Derscheid left us.

Chapter XVIII

Back to Kabale

WE NOW PREPARED TO CARRY OUT Carl Akeley's last project: a trip to Lake Hannington in Kenya, for material to build the greater koodoo group. Akeley had intended to undertake this on his return from the Congo, and we had decided to go on with his plan as if he were still with us.

The march from Rutchuru back to Uganda was somewhat strenuous; I always outdistanced all the rest because it is hard for me to walk slowly. At the boundary line between the Belgian Congo and Uganda the trail makes a right angle, and a lone tree stands at the turn, surrounded by rolling, grassy hills. Near this spot is a typical rest station built by the English—clean, whitewashed, empty. We had followed this trail upon our entry into the region—there was no other; nevertheless because I was traveling in the opposite direction, things looked different. Reason told me I could not be wrong, yet I was not satisfied. A big black man tending a herd of fat-tailed sheep stood near the tree. I summoned my best Swahili to address him.

"*Mpaka Belgi hii?*" (Is this the border of Belgium?)

"*Ndio.*" (Yes.)

Still I hesitated.

"*Wapi maji anguka?*" (Where is the waterfall?)

198

The man waved down the trail ahead of me; I was reassured.

It neared three o'clock, and I was hungry. In a yam field I saw a woman hoeing. She was a round-faced, black-brown stalwart.

I said to her, *"Ni taka ndizi."* (I would like to have some bananas.)

She stared at me, as I repeated my statement, dropped her hoe, and ran away. I plodded on, still hungry. I had not gone far when I heard someone calling, *"Bwana! Bwana!"*

I turned, and saw the woman with two men. The latter wore clean white cotton robes that fell to the ground, and white turbans. Shorter than the woman, they had cinnamon-colored skins and slender, refined, aquiline features. The woman was holding a flat basket piled with bananas.

I returned, and greeted the party with a smile. *"Jambo?"* (How are you?)

I selected half a dozen bananas.

"Kiasi gani?" (How much?)

"Shillinge moja." (One shilling.)

I realized that the two men belonged to the upper-caste Arab conquerors, who own everything in Uganda, and that the woman was an aborigine.

To my *"Ahsante sana"* (Thank you) and extended hand, the older man smiled, and gave me a long, delicate-fingered hand which had never done any work.

"Kwa heri!"

"Kwa heri!"

I now guessed that the woman had run away because she did not understand what I had said to her; she had simply repeated the sounds, so her master, who understood what they meant and owned the bananas, had supplied my want.

By five o'clock, I reached the resthouse at the waterfall in the Rutchuru River, pretty tired. One of the Arab aristocrats came up to me and asked when Mr. Akeley would arrive. I had to make the best fist I could of answering him:

"*Bwana Akeley akafa.*" (Mr. Akeley is dead.)

I felt that I was not saying it right, but it was the best I could do. The man looked puzzled; he asked questions which I only partly understood and could not answer.

I went down to the edge of the river; the green water was boiling and swirling most invitingly; the man had accompanied me.

"*Nitaka aga!*" (I would like to bathe!) I said.

"*Hapana, bwana; mamba!*" (No, Master, do not; crocodiles!)

So I removed only my shoes and puttees, and bathed my feet.

It was after six o'clock before the rest of the party caught up.

All the following day we traveled a level valley floor, and stopped at the resthouse in the middle of it that evening. The local chief had a bright little boy about nine years old, who was fired with an ambition to accompany us, so Mrs. Akeley allowed him to go on to Lake Hannington with her, promising to send him back to his parents afterwards.

The next day brought us once more to the top of the narrow ridge at Behungi. As we were walking along the backbone of the ridge, shortly before reaching the

resthouses, and were walled in by bamboo on both sides,
a disturbance in the thicket attracted our attention. We
paused. Suddenly a man about forty years old lurched
out of the jungle into the trail. He was almost completely naked, covered with dirt and blood, and wildly
distraught. He stood before us trembling, barely able to
speak.

We finally made out that he and a companion had
been cutting bamboo about two hundred yards from the
road, preparatory to building a hut. An elephant had
charged them and killed his friend, while he, knocked
down amid a lot of broken bamboo, crawled under it and
had miraculously escaped. Nobody would venture into
the bamboo to make a try at recovering the dead man's
body. Bill absolutely forbade any such attempt; he knew
the danger better than any of us.

We went on to the resthouse, and I was standing looking at the magnificent view—one of the finest in the
world—while the boys put up the tents, when two natives, streaming with perspiration and frightened half
to death, ran into camp, and dropped down panting.
When they could speak they told us that they had been
traveling with two companions along the trail at the foot
of the bamboo ridges, when elephants charged from the
bamboo and killed the other two.

Bill told me the elephants were unusually vicious here
because the natives make a practice of stealing up on
them and shooting them with poisoned arrows.

The elephant's technique of attack is first to fell his
victim with a blow from his trunk. He then kneels and
gores the prone form with his tusks, after which he
macerates it with his front feet. Next he picks up what

Elephant attacking natives in Uganda

remains of his enemy and flings it seventy-five or a hundred feet away. Finally he walks around in a circle for perhaps two hours, watching to see if the victim stirs. If it does, he returns to gore it again. This last peculiarity of waiting to see if his victim is dead makes it dangerous to approach the body of an elephant's kill until a good many hours have passed. Nothing but luck had prevented just such an attack on our party, when we traveled this same dangerous trail.

That night passed calmly. The dawn came with all the dewy sparkle and brilliant loveliness of a glorious, shimmering, tropical morning, with the songs of birds, the dance of butterflies, and the long floating feathers of shimmering mist veiling the valley far below. The harsh facts of the preceding evening seemed incredible.

The sun was only a little way above the eastern ramparts of pearly haze when we started down the long winding trail toward the ancient lakes. The porters moved at a dogtrot, their slender black forms, each with his load, strung out in line. Bill and I followed with our rifles.

The leading porters had disappeared behind a small pyramidal ridge when we heard a great uproar—yells and screams.

Realizing regretfully that either Bill or I should have been in the lead, we dashed forward, but nothing serious had happened. The porters had sighted some elephants, and had raised a big hullabaloo to scare them. The beasts had promptly made off into the bamboo. Soon after, we passed what the cheetahs had left of the two dead men. Nobody lingered.

We reached Lake Bunyoni that evening, dog-tired.

Bunyoni is one of a chain of lakes, and if a great poet had sought to contrive sheer, unrivaled loveliness, never in his most inspired moment could he have improved on this. Here were shadowy expanses of shore and its reflection, all in a scheme of silver, lilac and sage green. Zones of lily pads and blue lotus blossoms alternated with patches of papyrus, cattails, and feather grass. White geese floated on the quiet waters; grebe, ibis, and Kavirondo crane waded or winged in long lines, and wild duck moved in and out among the clumps of reeds, piloting their downy, darting broods. Burnished fish leapt, breaking the smooth surface into swift circles that flashed and melted into the dim reaches of sapphirine light.

We ferried across Lake Bunyoni, and camped on the Kabale side for the night. The next day we reached Kabale, seven miles from Lake Bunyoni. It was decided that I should go on to the papyrus swamps below the hill upon which the Kabale station stands, and make a study of this interesting growth. We were going to need three or four days to overhaul our trucks, load them, and organize the trip to Lake Hannington.

I therefore took one truck with my belongings, and drove down to a bridge spanning the stream at the center of the swamp. With a cook, his two helpers, and my tent boy, I established myself on the edge of the swamp, and immediately set to work.

As usual, I was an object of peculiar and never-flagging interest to the local population. A group of seven or eight women and girls gathered from nowhere and gaped in whispering absorption at everything I had or did. The bridge was wooden and, though substantial

Sacred ibis

enough, somewhat ancient. I sat on the edge of it so that
I could look upstream along a vista of papyrus, and I
found this the only place where any adequate view of
the swamp growth could be obtained.

For some reason unknown to me there were no mosquitoes in this swamp, and after supper I sat watching
the blood-red sun go down over the feathery papyrus,
while, still as death, a pair of ibis flew low over the tufted

205

growths, black against the red. I heard the note of a Kavirondo crane.

The next morning the whole cavalcade arrived from Kabale in the three trucks: Raddatz, Mrs. Akeley, and a hired native driver. A temporary driver followed with the Buick, which I was to drive.

Camp was quickly broken, and we were on our way.

During the afternoon we reached a wide swamp across which a straight, narrow earth road had been constructed, lifting us not more than two feet above the water. To keep the road from washing away, it had been piled high in the middle. This ridge was wet with rain when we reached it, and as slippery as if it had been coated with soft soap. In the middle of the swamp was a wooden bridge.

The trucks started out gingerly, like tightrope walkers. I came last. I had their tracks before me, with eloquent slippings and skiddings as warnings. I remembered walking the top rail of a fence as a barefoot boy— this had that skinned a mile. Of all the skittish balancing I ever did in my life, straddling that streak of gray clay —that squashed and malformed road—certainly took the cake. I don't know yet how I got time to breathe.

All of a sudden everything stopped. I bawled out an inquiry, and word came back by way of the line of porters resting atop of the truckloads, that the bridge was down.

We could not turn around; to back out was unthinkable! I climbed out, sloshed ahead, and found Mrs. Akeley, Raddatz, and our headman shaking dubious heads; the bridge had sunk in the middle of the span; if it remained in that position we might be able to get the machines across. We got down and piled a lot of big rocks under the bridge to keep it from sinking any lower. Then we piled stones under the up-tilted ends of the planks, so the wheels of the machines could climb them. Raddatz took a long look and a fresh chew of tobacco, settled himself in his seat, and stepped on the gas. With bated breath we watched the truck dive down, climb up, and—clear the bridge! A great sigh of relief! I got back to my car, and put it in first. As the last truck cleared the bridge I followed; of course it was easy for my lighter vehicle.

We now entered a treeless region of small clay mountains, with smooth bold lines, all covered with green grass. Here and there we passed a village of grass huts and banana orchards. The natives were a mild-mannered, brown people, scantily clad.

The next day we bowled along over a wide level plain, with a wide, straight road before us. Toward the evening we halted for a few minutes in a village. Here, as in all the other towns on any road, the Hindu merchant was conspicuous.

When the trucks started again, I tried to follow but found my car would not move. My starter was out of commission.

By this time night was upon us. But we knew there was a rest station ten miles from the village. The trucks were out of sight before I could get started by cranking.

That night must have been the blackest since the beginning of time; the road was narrow, the roadbed crooked and rough. Dense bushes extended for miles on either side. My horn didn't work; the inside light was

207

out—but my headlights were good. I found the gearshift by instinct, the brake bar the same way.

It was ideal country for buffalo, rhinoceros, and elephant. How nice it would be if we met one of these! Animals are apt to be dazzled by headlights, as I had found out when driving in Arizona, where coyote allowed themselves to be almost run over. But to run over a rhino, buffalo, or elephant would be a different matter. An auto horn might startle these customers, but human voices yelling would not impress them in the least.

About ten o'clock we reached the rest station and found it empty, so I concluded our trucks had gone on to the next station, ten miles beyond. The road became more crooked and rough, the country wilder. Big moths dashed against my windshield. Hyenas howled. A bushbuck ran across the road; some kind of bird gave out a dismal wail. I speculated as to whether a lion would molest an automobile. . . .

It was twelve o'clock, and I was benumbed, semisomnolent, when a dim flash of lightning, without thunder, revealed some huts. We had reached the second rest station. It was deserted.

We piled out, and my tent was up in a jiffy, and food prepared. I was too tired to eat much, but not too tired to note that our canny native driver would not leave his truck but made his bed in it. He had been following behind me: the other trucks were ahead: but were now lost to us.

I got up as the sun rose, but told the boys to be in no hurry with breakfast. I was convinced the trucks were behind us. And sure enough, at about seven-thirty, they rolled in. They had gone down a side road by mistake, had seen us pass by, but could not attract our attention. With daylight they had started to overtake us.

The next day we reached the ferry at Jinga, and crossed an arm of Lake Victoria Nyanza.

Four days later we came to the end of the road, at the Evans sisal farm on the floor of the Rift Valley. We all were ready to pile into bed immediately after eating a little food. We remained here for two days, while Raddatz overhauled our machines, and arranged everything so they could safely be left standing for some weeks, covered with wagon sheets, in the grass by the side of the road. The rest of our journey would have to be on foot.

When the day arrived to march we crossed the little river on a native bridge, and began to trudge along a well-defined trail. As we started, some of the porters headed off at right angles and had to be called back. I inquired at the time why the porters had started up that rough, steep hill strewn with boulders, but was told they were wrong.

I fell into my natural swinging stride which carries me ahead of other people. In consequence I was soon alone—ahead even of the porters, who go at a dogtrot—and I kept wondering why those porters had wanted to take the other trail. At last I met a native herder with about three hundred sheep and goats. I asked him, *"Wapi maji mcubwa?"* (Where is the big water?) He pointed off at right angles to the trail. It confirmed my suspicion that we were walking parallel with the lake, not toward it. We were a good many miles from the only trail that traversed the very rough country separating us from our goal. It was a bad trail, and we would have to retrace our steps, which I felt sure the others would not agree to do. But I did not hurry on at once. My herder was following his flock down a rough embankment into a shallow canyon. I noted with interest that here, too, the goats were exactly the same flecked and pied animals that the Navahos have. I had painted numerous studies of them at Keams Canyon, Arizona.

At the bottom of the canyon stagnant pools lay among the rocks, and about them the animals crowded, in dense masses. In the perpendicular wall of the canyon, just beyond them, I noted curious cavities of irregular size and shape, some of them as much as ten feet deep. I was not kept long in doubt as to their origin; for as soon as their thirst was quenched the animals began surging into these cavities, and licking at the soft rock. It contained salt; its outer surface, exposed to the air and elements, was hard, but inside it was scarcely firmer than hard clay. I wondered how many thousand years it had required for the little soft tongues of goats and sheep to honeycomb the rock.

About one o'clock I halted in fine shade at the edge of a brook to rest and eat my lunch, and the rest of the party caught up.

About four I found myself again far ahead. I paused, looking down into a rocky canyon bed, paralleling the trail. The prospect had a familiar look, and I realized that it reminded me of Yellowstone Park. I climbed down to the handsome pools of green water that lay amid deep crevices in blue granite, and thrust in a hand. Sure enough, the water was warm—like bath water! In fact, it was a ready prepared bath, inviting me. I lost no time in taking off my clothes and stepping in. I wallowed about, splashing and spluttering, but as I did so I noticed the peculiar odor that pervades geysers. Yes, it was sulphur, and other things too, and probably alkali—I tasted the stuff and grimaced.

Two hours later I found myself at a camp site, where I stretched out in the grass until the others arrived. I think we must have covered twenty miles that day: everybody was exhausted.

Chapter XIX

The Lake

THE NEXT MORNING an hour's walk brought us suddenly to a perfectly flat, open expanse of sand and clay. Five miles away a dense forest of palms appeared. It was a strange spectacle; evidently, this was a lake bed part of the season. We became conscious of a distant hum in the air, so faint that we paid it little heed. But presently the sound reasserted itself. We turned to the right, climbed a gentle slope, and suddenly came in sight of a broad burnished sheet of shimmering water—Lake Hannington. On it lay bright pink patches, each one about a mile long—flamingos!

A few miles away stood the thousand-foot escarpment of the Rift Valley, a background of pearl and wistaria that the glassy water reflected. It formed one tonal mass with the lake whose shore line was scarcely discernible. Against this the regiments of millions upon millions of flamingos receded in straight military lines, the pattern they made on the surface of the water indicating the depth limit at which they could feed. Each line of birds gradually narrowed as it trailed off in perspective, and their conch-shell reflections twinkled across the shining tide in infinitely delicate gradations, until only a bare thread of luminous pink-opal melted into the pale sapphire distance. The coralline armies were fishing, standing thigh-deep in the water, their heads and necks sub-

212

Flamingos at Lake Hannington

merged, their crooked, specialized beaks on the bottom. Some, with their heads raised for air, kept up a continuous hum of conversation.

As we appeared, a vast cloud of them took flight, like a flurry of snowflakes churned into the sunlit air by a gust of wind, but the fugitives made no apparent gaps in the ranks of those that remained, with only their bodies showing above the water and packed as close together as stones in a wall.

We all sat down at the edge of the lake. The birds that had risen streamed out in ribbons and loops miles long, gradually circling back and once more settling down. New flights of flamingos kept arriving from the southern end of the lake to join the hosts already on the feeding ground. Their honking clatter vibrated in the distance.

A gem of unique splendor in Africa's crown, this turquoise and coral lake lay magically beautiful; yet surely a subtle suspicion of treachery lurked in the pervading odor that tainted the air.

Limpid wavelets caressed the green-white pebbles on the shore at our feet; too gently pulsating even to lisp, they piled up long lines of fluffy foam that wound with the sinuous outline of the shore in fleecy ribbons, to right and left, and bore, bobbing toward us, red feathers, besides a dead flamingo. I picked the latter out of the water; as I did so I discovered the lake water was tepid and had the same warm, sickish flavor of sulphur, soda, and alkali that I had noticed in my bath water. I touched my finger to my tongue; the water was briny.

To our left lay the bare sand flats, and the distant palm forest surrounding a smaller lake which in the wet season merged with Hannington. Neither lake has any outlet. Bill informed me that buffalo and "very bad" elephant dwelt in that palm forest.

Lake Hannington extended to our right in the shadow of the Laikipia escarpment. It is claimed that the lake is only 20 miles long, but it looked longer than that to me, and it took us two days to walk to the other end. I observed along its shore many jets of white steam drifting lazily upward—hot springs, I thought.

We were aiming for the southern end of the lake, opposite the point at which we had arrived. Had we followed the porters that first morning, instead of calling them back, we would have saved ourselves—and them— a good long walk, but I have always been glad that we did not follow them, for it resulted in one of the most interesting experiences of my life.

When we again got under way we followed the shore of the lake. I forged ahead, as usual, lured ever on and on by beckoning marvels that revealed themselves in endless succession. I was toting my own gun. My boy, who carried my canteen of water, couldn't keep up with me, and dropped back. I did not object, since I enjoy the savor of the wilds.

The shore of the lake was indented here and there with little bays and promontories where streams—now dry —joined the lake. Ahead of me a particularly large plume of white steam kept boiling up and drifting away, to be dissipated in the dry sparkling air. I passed dead trees standing at various distances out in the water, sometimes a hundred, two hundred, three hundred feet. All were large, and all were dead. Their stark forms, from which the bark had generally dropped off, gleamed white, like skeletons. There was quite a variety, and they stood in rows, obviously marking what had once been the shore of the lake. Now there were no such trees living, anywhere in sight.

Along the present shore line there were no growths at all, rarely even water weeds. A broad band of grass lay between the lake and the scattering of scrubby acacia forest. All of this indicated that the level of the water had been lower, and that its former shores had been permanent for a long time. The great trees had grown on dry land at the edge of the water. Forty years earlier, when J. W. Gregory visited this lake, he saw these trees with withered leaves still on them. It occurred to me that perhaps the chemical content of the water had been different at that time, for now not a vestige of vegetation grew anywhere along the margin. The water would have killed the trees, by flooding them, but why did no other trees sprout? Had chemicals poisonous to such trees been added to the water?

The level of the lake might have been lowered by sudden seismic action, or the quantity of inflowing water may have been increased: the latter seems less probable. It looked to me as if the water were gradually rising, however; I saw no old shore lines anywhere. I became thirsty and stopped at a pool of clear water held in a rock basin, but when I tasted it, I got a shock; it tasted like the lye that is used in soap.

Farther on I found a spring that was almost boiling hot. I dipped my finger in the lake water and tasted that: it was undrinkable. Noon came; the rest of the party were far behind, so I did not wait—I was not hungry, anyhow. My only problem was water. At the

Flamingos at Lake Hannington

edge of the lake in little bays or creek ends algae made the water blood red. Farther out on the lake long serpentine streaks of lettuce-green scum made ornate patterns on the glassy surface. The shadowy reflection of the opposite escarpment and the inverted cloud billows added witchery to the color scheme. Hundreds of stones along the shore had been recently turned over by baboons looking for insects. In some of the bays large numbers of geese, crane, duck, ibis, and smaller waders floated above their reflections, or fished along the sand bars.

As evening approached, I reached a point where a great number of springs had changed the nature of the ground. The ordinary vegetation had vanished and given place to a short, dense, plushlike dark-green grass. This formed a thick sod, through which little slits and furrows wound, brown-red and filled with swiftly running hot water. I searched, testing dozens of them, and walking up the incline. Finally I saw two native women filling their gourds. I made for the spot and found the only drinkable water I had tasted all day. I knew the rest of the party would be famished for water, so I sat down to wait for them. While I waited a flock of guinea fowl and two more native women came to drink: evidently this was the best water in the neighborhood.

Mrs. Akeley, Raddatz, and Bill arrived in about an hour's time, with the porters straggling behind. We made camp. While we were at supper, after sundown, large flights of flamingos kept passing northward toward the great feeding grounds we had seen that morning. We observed three hippopotamus out in the lake. The great creatures, which always impressed me as the

most beastly beasts of all I know, saw us and would not
come ashore, for they are cunning; I had heard that they
were in this lake, yet after tasting its water I wondered
how they could live there. While these thoughts absorbed
me, Mrs. Akeley suggested that Bill take the shotgun
and try for one of the geese at the edge of the lake. Having no cover, Bill missed the birds, yet even before he
fired, the wily hippos submerged, without a sound or a
ripple.

Morning dawned clear and brilliant, and as soon as
breakfast was over, we were off again. About ten o'clock
I reached the big boiling spring, whose steam I had seen
all along.

A maelstrom of savagely boiling water roared up end-
lessly, gushing over the edges of the chimney built by its
own sediment during periods of less eruptive fury. The
steam escaped with a loud hiss while the water belched
out of one principal vent and many smaller ones. Sedi-
mentary stone—solidified deposit—shelved out over the
many little torrents that rushed from the caldron to
meet on the lake side of the fountain and gallop in tem-
pestuous and venomous wrath down the scoriac incline
of smoking rocks. The typical geyser smell—that sickish
compound of sulphur, lime, alkali, soda, and what-not
all boiling together—filled my nostrils, and all the rocks
were hot under my feet. No cold water flows into Lake
Hannington; hot springs surround it; plumes of steam
line the lake's entire length on both sides.

At the hot spring a shallow fold in the hills began,
and a trail led away from the lake obliquely toward the
south. We had agreed to follow the shore of the lake,

and nothing had been said to me about branching off at this point.

After taking some photographs, and waiting until the rest of the party were in sight, I waved my pith hat to them. They answered with wavings of arms and hats. I naturally continued to follow the shore of the lake.

As I advanced, the shore became higher and rockier; more patches of thornbush appeared, and diminutive bushbuck darted in and out. I had for a long time seen what I thought was the end of the lake, but I began to suspect it was merely a long cape extending out into the water, and that the lake continued on beyond it. My guess was soon to be verified: as the shore rose, and cliffs began to line the water, I was forced to pursue a course farther from the shore.

Lake Hannington is briny at the northern end and brackish at the southern. The green scum on its surface are floating algae, and the turbid water beneath this scum exhales an effluvium that is rather nauseating. Yellowstone Park contains a pond called Turbid Lake, which is always muddy from the activity of subsurface boiling springs. I suspected the same conditions here.

The thornbushes became so thick that I could not escape them entirely. My helmet and shirt were sadly scarified and full of holes; numerous scratches oozed blood on my arms and face. The sun was hot as a furnace, and the water I had hoped to find did not materialize. This was becoming a serious question; we can do without food but not without water. Of course, I found springs and rock-pocket pools, some green, some yellow, and some vermilion, but they all swarmed with wrigglers, skimmers, and flies, and they were all warm and fetid.

At last I arrived at the edge of a deep rocky canyon, at the bottom of which I saw a pool. Down I plunged to the side of the heaven-sent basin, in the midst of a sandy depression at the foot of a dry waterfall. Half the water had evaporated from the pool, leaving a band of rotting scum a foot wide all around it, and innumerable dead flies and beetles. A dead mouse floated in the center. What had killed these creatures? I didn't drink.

Making my way to the foot of a large tree where there was clean sand and good shade, I stretched myself out on my back, and half closed my eyes. I was hot, wet, and tired, and the ragged crags and writhing vine above, with the sun's light like gold dust sifting through, turned the world into a drowsy half-real, half-dream mirage. I heard a strange jumble of sounds and opened my eyes. A rowdy rout of birds of many kinds, headed by a crow, had discovered me; they thought I was dead. The garrulous mob included many shapes, sizes, and colors. Some of the smaller ones exhibited surprising curiosity and came within easy reach of my hand. On the trunk of the tree a gray lizard was enjoying the unseemly racket, but several hyrax on near-by rock shelves were scandalized. A green monkey in the top of an adjoining tree expressed in vehement terms his unqualified disapproval. The birds thought it was time to begin feasting on my remains, but the hyrax and monkey suspected I was still alive.

I started up; the mob vanished. An hour had passed. "Fool!" I said to myself, "it could just as easily have been hyenas, or a leopard!"

I sprang to my feet, gun in hand.

Up the canyon a tangle of rocks, trees, and vines already in shadow told of a declining sun; it looked dark and mysterious, as if anything might lurk there. Down the canyon a vista gave a glimpse of the lake; the walls of the gulch on the far side were more broken—could I climb them? I managed it without much trouble, and pursued my way on level ground.

As I neared a heap of rocks and bushes, a startling crash and scurry brought me to a halt. A huge wart hog stood not more than twenty paces away. With his tremendous tusks curving up, his gargoyle head covered with knobs and excrescences, his splotchy skin straggled over with long russet hairs, he contemplated me through little red eyes. His tail—his danger signal—stood rigidly erect. My rifle was in readiness, my finger ready to touch the trigger, but the hog decided to make off.

Klipspringer and dik-dik darted across my path; impala bounded over the rocky ridge above me; a fox barked, and then bolted.

I neared the point where the peninsula jutted out into the lake, and my game path brought me down near the edge of the lake. A big black herder was tending a bunch of goats drinking tepid water in a swampy stretch of ground.

I was about ready to tackle anything wet, so I approached the herder.

"*Jambo.*" I doubted whether he understood Swahili, and was delighted when he replied, "*Jambo, bwana!*"

"*Maji hii mzuri?*" (Is this water good?) I demanded, indicating the tracks.

"Hapana, bwana, mbaya sana!" (No, sir, it is very bad!)

"Kuja." (Come.)

He conducted me through an acacia grove, across the neck of the peninsula, to an expanse of denuded red soil, deeply furrowed by dry stream beds, which, where they merged with the lake, became a reedy marsh teeming with ibis and herons. Beyond the earth stretch a green zone appeared. Here another herd of goats were drinking.

My guide pointed with his spear.

"Maji mzuri," he said.

"Ahsante sana." (Thanks very much.)

I gave him a shilling.

"Kwa heri!"

I hastened to the point he indicated. Among a great number of seep springs, mostly warm, I found issuing from beneath a large rock one which was almost cool, besides being free from salt, alkali, and soda. Before I had finished drinking, flat on my stomach, I was surrounded by goats. They knew good water from bad as well as I did, and wanted to drink immediately beside me. I objected by pushing their noses away, but they were in no wise afraid and continued to nose and jostle me. There was plenty of water, but mine was the best; it came out over sand and pebbles, translucent and purling from under the rock. Hundreds of bees and wasps also knew that my water hole was the best, and refused doggedly to be driven away; they, the goats and I, patched up a gentlemen's agreement to take turns at drinking. As soon as I had drunk my fill, I sat on the rock while the goats clustered about; I sat amid a sea

Flamingos and pelicans at Lake Hannington

of goats while a scantily clad and grinning aborigine looked on.

But presently a hoodlum gang of baboons appeared on the rocky ridge just above. One old shaggy patriarch challenged me furiously, but when I suddenly leaped up, he almost broke his neck, stampeding over his wives and children.

They were this side of a rocky island, crowned with bushes, that looked like a gem set in a brooch. Its boulders, painted at the base with a yard-wide band of gypsum tinged cream-gold by the sun, shimmered ineffably. I had time to observe it all, for I sat there a long time.

Why didn't the rest of my party catch up?

The declining sun cast orange shafts that splintered and tumbled over the clump of trees behind me. All about in a scintillant blaze the old-rose glory flooded; it wantoned along the purple escarpment, five miles distant, that closed in the southern end of the lake.

I sat—or rather I wandered away in fancy on excursions into the beckoning canyons and jungles. In imagination I was skimming the rugged summits in an airplane, flitting over those jagged far crags like a swallow, when, crash! Two reverberating rifleshots recalled me to the present.

The shots sounded as if they had come from about the neighborhood of the canyon where I had taken my nap.

I quickly fired two shots in answer.

Was it a signal? Maybe those shots had been fired at something!

Had they really come from the direction of the canyon—or from some other spot?

Chapter XX

Night with an African Shepherd

I HASTENED BACK across the peninsula; the herder and his goats were gone. Where the swampy zone jutted out into the lake a hundred yards, I hurried out to its tip to obtain a view of the shore line. I hoped to see someone of our party approaching, but no one appeared. I saw only a wisp of steam from the big spring, and heard a lone jackal bark. Just as I reached the water's edge, a tremendous splashing startled me, and an immense hippopotamus stood within thirty feet of me. He had been lying in the shallow water where a few cattails grew; I, with my attention fixed on the shore line and hills, had not seen him; he, asleep, had not seen me until I got very close. I jerked my rifle into position, and there we stood, each staring at the other.

The animal, after a hasty but careful survey of me, decided I was an unneighborly interloper, and, with snorts of suspicion and disgust, moved out into deep water.

I continued my retreat; a hyena skulked off with ungainly motions and mean and treacherous backward scowls. In a dusty place I came upon the track of a leopard.

The sun, a blood-red globe amid far-flung shafts of molten gold, reddened the purple ridges as it sank. De-

Author and hippopotamus

spite my haste I paused a moment to observe its orgy of barbaric crimson grandeur!

I reached the brink of the canyon; its depths were already filling with gloom. I suddenly became aware of a sheep standing within ten feet of me, also gazing down into the gorge. "What a strange thing!" I said to myself. "The creature is lost!"

I hastened along the brink, away from the sheep, up broken rock benches, to a bend in the gorge; below me appeared the tops of big, dense trees, and a wild racket burst out. I had startled a lot of baboons and green monkeys. One old male leapt from a crag to a tree, where, for a moment he remained, cursing me rabidly, while his family scampered out of sight. I judged they had been preparing to make their beds for the night on the flat floors of leaves and vine-matted branches.

It behooved me also to look for a place to spend the night. The prospect was not very inviting, especially when I recalled the hyena and the leopard's tracks.

A big owl started up below me, and some vultures were routed from their perches among the trees by the stampeding baboons.

There might be a variety of marauders lurking in the obscurity of the canyon jungle, and this was the prowling hour.

There would be no purpose in crossing the canyon, even had it looked less forbidding. At the same time, the prospect of spending the night on these bare, high rocks, without water—I was thirsty again—and without food, did not inspire me with enthusiasm.

I went through all my pockets; not a single match. Most of us have grown up with the idea that fire frightens wild animals. I have heard experienced hunters dispute this. But in any case a fire would yield cheer and warmth. It was growing cold.

One never realizes in daylight how completely human beings depend on sight, but at night the truth is driven home.

The moon was still low. I found myself sensitive to every slightest sound: the chirp of insects, the stirring of a fitful breeze among the trees; and I became conscious of the inadequacy of the ear for protection.

As I stood on the brink of the abyss, I again heard the long wail of a hyena from not far away. Probably the one I had seen had followed me. It was the immemorial cry of protest of the outcast—the desperate—of hunger-driven ferocity.

What should I do?

Seeking an answer to this question, I chanced to look across the gorge and discovered on the opposite side a man—a tall, black man, already some distance from the canyon, and moving away. I had never expected to be so glad to see a naked savage.

I shouted.

The man turned and began retracing his steps. As he descended into the gulch I perceived he was making for the place where I had climbed out of it; I went to meet him.

I told myself as he approached that this savage was going to be my host for one night.

As he climbed up to where I stood I saw that he was slender, and of a deep coffee color. His costume consisted of a piece of plain calico, originally white, over one shoulder, and depending on one side to the middle of his thigh. As adornment he wore earrings and a cord of sinew around each wrist; he also wore sandals and carried a herder's spear.

"*Jambo?*"

"*Jambo!*" with a deferential intonation. It was up to me to marshal all the Swahili at my command.

"*Wapi nyumba yako?*" I asked. (Where is your house?)

He repeated the word "*nyumba.*" Evidently he did not know much Swahili. I changed the question.

"*Wapi boma yako?*" (Where is your corral?)

"*Boma—boma?*" he puzzled.

"*Wapi shamba yako?*" (Where is your field?)

He looked at me blankly, as well he might, since, in this world of lava beds, fields or gardens—tillage—were quite unknown.

I was becoming desperate! What if communication between us should prove impossible?

"*Wapi lala?*" I ventured. (Where do you sleep?)

Ah! His face brightened; he understood. He pointed across the gorge toward the top of the ridge in which the canyon made a gash. Encouraged by this success, I propounded another pertinent question:

"*Ulisekia bunduki leo?*" (Have you heard a gunshot today?) Again he was mystified.

"*Hii bunduki*" (This is a gun), I said, shaking the gun before him.

Ah! He comprehended.

"*Vema, nilisekia, Bwana; m'bili!*" (Yes, sir, I heard it twice!)

He pointed across the gulch once more, this time toward the hot spring.

So I was right. The party could not be very far away, probably a mile at the most.

Now I had a burning question to ask.

"Wapi maji mzuri?" (Where is good water?)

He pointed down into the black depths of the gorge. Then he, too, asked a question.

"Ulitazama kando?" (Have you seen a sheep?)

"N'dio!" (Yes!)

I led him to the point where I had seen the sheep; but, alas, the beast had vanished.

"Chakula kwa fisi!" (Food for hyenas!) remarked my friend regretfully, as he glanced resignedly about at the thornbushes in the fast-growing darkness. He turned to the higher ledges of bare rock, to the point where I had been when I frightened the baboons, and led to the highest part. I looked down into blackness where tree snags and rocks protruded and bats flew about. Something that might have been a frog sent up a quavering squawk from the inky obscurity, and the old baboon grandfather grumbled imprecations, I fancied.

The African began the descent into this Hades by a trail the like of which Dante never dreamed of. My guide was very careful to draw attention to shaky stones, and to deep drops over precarious ledges into ever profounder pools of gloom.

In some wonderful way we reached the bottom, only about a hundred or a hundred and fifty yards above where I had taken my nap, but how it had changed. The night had marvelously transformed the place; its sunny, peaceful aspect by daylight could only be guessed at.

My guide halted amid the fantastic wilderness of

231

rocks, roots, trunks, and vines, and pointed to something at his feet, as I could dimly discern.

"*Maji mzuri,*" he said.

I joined him, and caught the gleam of a star in a black pool and the faint lisp of water.

"*Maji mzuri!*" repeated my guide.

I dropped on all fours, bent low, and drank; the water was cool and sweet.

Little secret sounds as of insects—little glimmers like elfin eyes—a dead leaf fell to the water's surface and floated past my nose.

"*Tuta kwnda?*" (Shall we be going?) I said, getting to my feet.

My host led the way up a branch canyon over a riot of rocks and roots and under fallen trees to the farther level of a comparatively smooth country. A mile and a half, dodging thornbushes, and stumbling amid loose stones, brought us to a goat corral where two boys awaited their father.

I had looked anxiously in all directions during our walk, for the campfire I expected to see, to lead me back to my friends, but all in vain. In a colloquy of which I understood not a syllable, the boys were informed concerning me. A part of it, apparently, had to do with the camp I was hoping to find, and I divined it was adverse to my hopes.

I asked the older boy the same question regarding the gunshot, and he at once replied affirmatively, but waved in the opposite direction from the hot spring. I wondered whether he had understood me correctly; I asked the smaller boy: the answer was the same.

At a suggestion from the father, the older boy asked,

"Wapi utalala usiku?" (Where will you sleep tonight?)

"Nita ka hapa." (I will remain here.)

They led the way up the ridge to a second *boma,* beside which stood a lone flat-topped tree. We were now high above the lake, near the crest of the rock-ribbed eminence, a bleak and barren spot, with scarcely a trace of soil upon the lava, with a sparse and wretched sprinkling of stunted thornbushes eking out a precarious existence.

The top of a grass hut loomed against the sky; a second thorn corral came in view. The hut stood in the center of the shamba, which was crowded with goats and sheep. The bucks were roughing it—jostling, banging, pushing, and fighting. The sound of clashing horns and trampling hoofs, the snort and sneeze and cough, the short impatient bleat of lambs and kids never ceased; and the acrid stench and clouds of rank dust never subsided.

I was wondering whether the *m'ke* (wife) was absent, when a melodious, feminine voice floated from the gloom and bedlam, and a woman emerged from the hut. She carried a baby on her back, and was preceded by a mongrel dog.

The sweet-voiced woman immediately was filled with kindly solicitude; the stranger must be cared for.

"Bwana nachoka?" (Is Master not tired?)

She spoke better Swahili than her husband.

"M'wanamke," I said, *"ulisikia bunduki leo?"* (Madam, did you hear a gun today?)

"N'dio, Bwana; nisikia bunduki m'bili, lakini, mbali sana!" (Yes, sir, I heard a gun twice, but it was very far away!)

She waved toward the south.

I was amazed. Evidently I had been deceived in my estimation of the sound, by the conformation of the hills deflecting it and had come in the wrong direction.

The woman's costume consisted of a skirt of leather falling from the waist to the knees, some brass rings around her ankles and wrists, and a wooden plug in each ear. The children were quite naked.

The woman re-entered the hut, and returned with a gourd in her hand.

"*Chakula kadogo?*" (A little food?) she suggested, proffering the gourd.

"Oh, *hapana! Siwezi kula!*" (Oh, I could not eat!) A thumping lie.

Visions of dysentery, typhoid, assailed me.

But this wise woman knew I had lied; she pressed the gourd into my hand.

"*Maziwa ya n'gombe; mzuri sa-a-a-a-na!*" It is the milk of the cow—very, very good!)

Her hospitality and her persuasive voice rendered further hesitation impossible: it would never do to offend my kind hostess.

Typhoid or no typhoid, it was good sour milk.

Then one of the boys brought another gourd.

"*Maziwa ya mbuzi; mzuri sa-a-a-a-a-ana!*" (Milk of the goat; extremely good!)

It was delicious and I needed it. I was becoming weak from hunger, having eaten nothing since breakfast.

The whole family, including the dog, now gathered around to get a really satisfying look at me. They had never had an opportunity before to examine that won-

derful thing—a white man, at close quarters; to handle
the things he carried and wore.

Of first interest to the family was my gun.

I showed them how it worked; how to place the butt
against the shoulder, and sight along the barrel. I took
out a clip and showed them the cartridges, explaining,
as best I could in my pidgin Swahili and pantomime,
how and why the bullets flew; and what made the noise.
They took it in their hands with reverent care and ex-
clamations of delight.

Next, my eyeglasses had to be inspected, and tried on
by every one in turn; only the dog refrained. They evidently thought there was something magical about the
lenses; this fearsome charm must be handled with cir-
cumspection.

Now the smallest boy discovered my fountain pen.

I took a dried goatskin lying near, and drew an elephant as best I could by the dim light of the rising moon.
As the drawing developed the oldest boy exclaimed,
"Tembo!" (Elephant!) Then a wave of excitement
swept the family; the smallest boy screamed with delight; only the dog and the baby remained unmoved.

Now the little fellow spied my watch chain, so I
hauled out the timepiece, detached it, and let him listen
to its ticking. Of course, it had to go the rounds of the
family, and, torn between curiosity and caution, the
grave father turned the terrific thing gingerly over and
over, trying to make out where the tick came from. He
listened and smelled it, he felt it and tasted it, and shook
his head in profound mystification.

"Hii, sa!" (This is time!) I said, and did my best to
explain. I pointed to the moon and then to the hands; I

indicated that when the moon had reached the opposite horizon, the hands would be at a different place. My efforts convinced them that the watch held inside of it a god or a devil.

My camera came next. I opened it, and explained, *"Sanamu"* (pictures). They would not touch that. Beyond doubt it would be imprudent to venture; the thing was unquestionably dangerous—probably diabolical!

Had I been an adept in Swahili I might, perhaps, have conveyed more sense to them, but certainly no more pleasure! They palpitated and shivered with delicious chills and shudders.

My pith helmet came next; it had to be fitted on every head—except the baby's and the dog's. The buttons on my clothes were fascinating, purely decorative, of course —most subtle and artful. When I demonstrated their utilitarian value, a shout of delight and wonder followed.

My shoes with shining hobnails in the soles, my intricate puttees, the soft hair on my arms (Africans have smooth arms and legs), the straight hair on my head, my mustache and the freckles on my arms and neck were decorations to marvel at.

I was on the verge of becoming conceited.

Then the little fellow found the hunting knife on my belt, which was in a scabbard of lion hide with the hair on. The head of the family pushed the child aside with patient prudence: he must not be too officious. When I drew the blade they exclaimed with admiration, but knives they knew—the scabbard was what caught their eyes.

"Simba" (lion), I explained. They recognized it; and

gasped with awe. I shot up to dizzy heights in their estimation—I was a mighty hunter!

They jumped to the conclusion that I had vanquished the king of beasts singlehanded. Had I done it with the knife? In their eyes, that weapon was far more formidable than any gun. I despaired of making them realize that I had not slain the lion at all. It was no use. I was a hero, a prodigy of valor!

Weariness began to invade my senses. I began to seek for a spot between the stones where I might lie with reasonable comfort.

"Utalala ndane kabonda?" (Will you not sleep in the house?) asked the woman, politely.

Having visions of vermin, I replied, suavely, *"Nita lala hapa."* (I will sleep here.)

The woman went inside and returned with another goatskin. I now had two skins, hairless, and as stiff as boards, but they were lifesavers. By arranging them so that they would shield me from the chilly breeze coming from the lake, and lying on the lower edges to keep them in place, they made it possible for me to rest without becoming chilled. I managed to find a place in the dust where only a few stones gouged me in the ribs.

In the band of light across the lake cast by the moon, five hippopotamus showed their heads above water. Across the moon a line of flamingos flew. Turning my back to the moon, I dropped into an uncomfortable reverie.

My host came out and lay down near me. He thought it prudent, in view of prowling hyenas. It was very gentlemanly of him; I appreciated it.

I woke soon after dawn as my hostess emerged from

the hut. For the first time I saw clearly the owner of the caressing voice. She seemed a frail little thing, with hardship written at the corners of her wanly smiling mouth. She was still young; her two round breasts were still handsome but had just begun to sag.

Flamingos flying across the moon. Hannington

"*Jambo, bibi!*" (Good morning, Madam!) I said, pressing a shilling into her hand, and shaking it at the same time.

She didn't know what the handshake meant, but she understood the shilling.

"*Jambo, bwana!*"

I picked up my gun and camera.

"*Utaneangozi*" (You will guide me), I said to the man.

"*N'dio.*" He picked up his spear.

The baby cried; the mother re-entered the hut, and

returned with the infant greedily taking his breakfast.
I gave the boys some coins, and the man and I hit the
trail.

"*Kwa heri!*" I called back, waving.

"*Kwa heri, bwana!*"

The mother, the two boys, and the dog stood looking
after us; only the baby was too busy to bother.

My guide was a master at dodging thornbushes. I was
interested in his methods because I had been less successful. I decided that his lack of clothing was one thing
in his favor; experience did the rest.

We reached the trail, which branched upward from
the hot spring and evaded the canyon. In the dust were
the clear marks of the automobile tire sandals of the
porters. It now became clear what had happened. The
rifleshots had really come from south of me, instead of
north, as I had thought. The conformation of the hills
may have been responsible, or was it due to my own
faulty observational powers?

An hour's walk brought us within sight of a densely
wooded depression, and above the trees arose a column
of smoke: the cook's campfire.

I learned that when they reached the camp site, Mrs.
Akeley had Raddatz fire the two shots I had heard. My
answering shots did not carry to where they were, so
they thought I must have been eaten.

I gave my new-found friend a good breakfast. I also
presented him with a shilling for each of the boys, not
forgetting the baby, another one for his wife, and two
for himself, besides two brightly colored bandanna handkerchiefs.

Chapter XXI

Up the Escarpment

OUR TEMPORARY CAMP proved to be situated on an island, in a forest of large trees. The grove was cut into many strips by numerous streams of warm water, all of which one could jump across.

Soon after breakfast we broke camp, and Bill, who had been here before with Akeley, led the way farther upstream, away from the lake, out of the forest, to a more comfortable camp site.

Here the stream had not yet split up into channels but flowed in one bed some twelve feet wide, except where it spread into reedy swamp patches. Native cattle grazed in the meadows, but near the water was long coarse grass that I knew cattle would not eat. Nevertheless, it had been unevenly cropped, and huge tracks appeared in the oozy mud. I called Bill's attention to this, and as I expected, he said, "Hippopotamus."

"So far from the lake?" I asked.

"Yes. They will wander as far as five or six miles during the night, in search of grass."

He was unquestionably right, for cattle could not make such tracks.

Hippopotamus are dangerous only under certain circumstances. When they are stampeded, far from the water, they will run down, or snap at anybody who tries to cut them off. A female will attack a canoe, or swim-

240

mer, that chances too close to where her calf lies under the surface of the water. In certain spots where many hippopotamus abound they are very bold, and will attack canoes and swimmers, apparently without cause.

At the camp we established here I saw, for the first time in Africa, houses built in trees. The purpose I could not ascertain. Some were granaries, I think, placed to protect the grain from damp and rats.

The day following our arrival here, after a consultation with Mrs. Akeley, I sorted out my equipment, and selected my carriers for an expedition to the top of the Laikipia escarpment of the Rift. There I planned to find a place to paint the study for the greater koodoo group as originally planned.

The greater koodoo and lesser koodoo are first cousins and resemble each other closely. When Akeley first visited this country these noble antelopes could still be found on the upper rim of the cliffs. But the English told us none remained. However, this was their natural habitat, a fit country in which to place them. This plan was later changed, as we shall see.

A young native, a very capable-looking fellow, was brought to me, and wanted to guide me to the top. But from where we were no suggestion of a trail could be seen. I asked him whether there was one. It seemed to me there should be, but he assured me there was not. I assumed he knew what he was talking about; there seemed no reason why he should lie. Nevertheless, I had a suspicion in the back of my head: I had learned from experience that natives had trails leading practically everywhere.

When we started the next morning, the guide led us

up the foothills, which grew continually more steep and difficult. The poor porters puffed and staggered; they bled and sweated uncomplainingly; still the guide advanced, on such precarious footing that even his bare feet slipped. The ground was covered with dead grass, long and brittle, and the dried stems lay flat on the ground, all pointing down hill, washed so by the rains. When a footing was sought on the clay incline carpeted with this grass, the latter broke off at the roots, and clinging like soft soap to the sole of the foot, formed toboggan slides. A more ingenious murder trap was never invented.

Yet, hanging on by his toes and fingers, he still called to the heavily loaded porters to follow.

We were nearing a precipice, so I called a halt. The men were nearly worn out, whereas the guide, with nothing to carry but himself, grinned cheerfully.

While the porters steadied themselves, and wiped away the sweat, I studied the surrounding slopes. It certainly was a wild and discouraging prospect, yet about a mile away the escarpment wall showed a series of breaks that looked as if it ought to be possible to scale the heights there. The longer I examined this place the more I became convinced there must be a way of getting up at that point.

I called the guide to me, and pointed.

"*Njia huko?*" (Is there not a trail there?) I asked.

"*Hapana, bwana!*" (No, sir!)

Well, this rascal, who professed to know the country intimately, and doubtless did, was not convincing to me. I told the porters to rest while I investigated. I had observed a yellowish line threading crookedly up the lower foothills; I determined to find out what it was. Yet I gave the guide another chance.

I pointed again.

"*Hii njia!*" (That is a path!) I insisted.

Persistently that barbarian shook his head in the negative.

I left the party where they were, with injunctions not to move until I came back. I descended to the level and made for the yellow streak, and as I neared it I saw some natives driving down a herd of goats. So I was right. It was a trail, well-worn. I ascended about six hundred feet over an exceedingly rough terrain, and reached a big halfway bench, or terrace. From here I could see that the cliffs beyond were still more fractured, and there was no doubt in my mind that the trail would conduct us to the summit.

I retraced my steps, and, when I had gotten within hailing distance, called to the porters to come down and follow me. The guide did not come with them. I never saw the rascal again.

By the time we regained the place where I had turned, the sun was low, and we were all dripping wet and caked with dust, besides being thoroughly scarified with thorns. I decided to make camp.

My tent was put up on a level spot and a nice little fire built before the sun went down. It was a very fine sunset, but I was in no mood to admire it. Some of the porters were so fagged out they dropped down to sleep without eating. I went to bed early and slept serenely.

The next morning, immediately after dawn, I took a hasty breakfast, grabbed my gun, and, bidding the boys wait for my return, started off up the trail. It was long and beastly rough but less steep than the section I had traversed the day before. By the tracks I knew that the natives brought cattle as well as goats up this trail.

Topping the final four hundred feet, I found the country sloping sharply down, away from the escarpment edge. The latter was a line of sharp, ragged, upstanding saw edges, hogbacks, irregular and difficult. But a short distance back of them the footing was quite decent. The red and chocolate-brown rocks tilted consistently down from the edge, so that a mile back the ground was from two to three hundred feet lower. From below I had picked out a notch in the rocky wall, which I anticipated would yield the view I was looking for.

I followed the line of hogbacks for some two miles and found myself in a gently sloping little valley, which led me to a notch in the ridge. I observed, looking over the edge, a precipitous trail descending amid boulders, and promised myself I would later descend to see what I might find.

I had reached an angle in the cliff walls, which from this point sheered off across the southern end of the lake, some two miles, and then turned again at an obtuse right angle, to continue along the eastern side.

There was a good game trail here and a superb view of the lake and of the Rift Valley, but for pictorial purposes I wanted to be in a depression with walls rising to right and left. So I pushed on, knowing that the notch I had picked out from below still lay ahead of me. Another short mile brought me to it: an ideal spot—just what I had hoped to find.

After briefly looking the place over, and deciding where I would place my working fly, I made my way back to camp. Three of my porters said they could carry all there was between them, and made three packages of it. The other five men I sent back to headquarters.

The journey back to my notch was tedious and uneventful. By night the fly and my tent were up, and everything ready. I began work about three o'clock, and had the most serious part of the drawing done by sunset.

About four o'clock every afternoon, as I sat at work, bands of baboons would arrive. I would become conscious of their presence, when their familiar denunciations, "Oh! Oh!" sounded. In the midst of my absorption, this bark would recall me to a consciousness of my surroundings, and I had only to turn my head to discover on a rock, or in the crotch of a tree, the old-man baboon. He would not be far away or far from the edge of the cliffs, and he would remain on the far side of my little valley, at the edge of the notch.

These animals travel regular rounds daily, hunting for edible roots, grass seeds, fruit, beetles, snails, worms, or birds' nests, so they encountered me at about the same time each day, as they followed their routine. I was an interruption to their habits, and they objected. Down in the little valley there were probably many crickets and grass seeds and other luscious titbits it was a shame to forego. But it would not do to venture too close to such an evil-looking interloper as I. All that was left them was to make a detour around me, and that was humiliating; and so, after spending half an hour telling me what they thought of me, they would go up to the far end of the little valley before crossing to my side. But invariably on the way the patriarch of the tribe could not resist the opportunity afforded by some convenient forked tree, to climb up and give me another tongue-lashing.

Chapter XXII

Back to Nairobi

ABOUT JANUARY 23, Mrs. Akeley and Raddatz came up to visit me. The former took some fine photographs, and the latter again tied his little pieces of cloth to a number of growths to mark those of which I was to make color notes after I finished my study of Hannington.

Mrs. Akeley planned a return to the north end of the lake, to take photographs of the flamingos. Raddatz and Bill, with their boys and equipment, were to accompany her. While on the escarpment, Raddatz collected a lot of bushes, plants, stones, and grass to be brought back with my things. I named a day when I would be finished with my work. On the morning of that day some extra porters would arrive, and I was to descend to the main camp, where I would find more porters and the baggage all packed. I was to rest for one night, and start the following morning for the Evans farm and the trucks.

On the appointed day, the extra native porters, who had been hired in advance, arrived.

Raddatz had invented and constructed a large wooden box in which my wet studies could be carried safe from dust or damage of any kind. It worked perfectly but was clumsy to transport. I slung it on a pole, so that two men could carry it between them.

It seems to me I have never painted a better study

247

than the Hannington one: the place appealed to me enormously. I hated to leave the camp, and I would welcome an opportunity to revisit the region. The time was drawing near when I would leave Africa—my Africa. I could not reconcile myself to the thought of being without my nightly hyena serenade.

We descended the escarpment and reached the lake side without any mishap. I found that the little boy Mrs. Akeley had brought from Kisola was still at the camp, in the care of the head cook; both had fever. For this reason they had not accompanied Mrs. Akeley. I gave them each quinine; the cook a ten-grain pill, the lad five grains. The little fellow insisted on chewing up his pill, in spite of all my remonstrances, but the effects were just as good. The drug helped them, and both reached Nairobi safely.

By five o'clock the following morning we were under way, a long line strung out over a quarter of a mile. The sun soon became very hot, but a good breeze was blowing, so travel was not unbearable.

There was not much of a trail to follow, and what there was soon became so confused with myriads of others, branching in every direction, that only a person acquainted with the country could have picked the right one. Of course, all our native porters knew it.

This trail soon led us up over a rough, broken layer of chocolate-colored lava a hundred feet thick, and beyond to the great stretches of rusty red, seminaked regions, where only stunted thornbushes, poverty grass, and a few dwarf acacias grew.

The terrain soon became broken and rough. In one canyon we dumped our loads on the earth, and the porters dug avidly in the sand, like animals in search of water. The thirsty men excavated until they came to a muddy fluid, but it was so filled with salt and alkali that it was undrinkable.

I had a *kabuyu* (canteen), but by this time it was empty. I was carrying it myself, for my former gun boy, Ibrahim, had joined a group who deserted us during our return from the Congo. But Kwambe, my careful tent boy, young and strong, and old Tomassie, had remained loyal.

Tomassie came from Lake Rudolf, and was of a different tribe from the rest of our men. He was an atheist! He was wholly uninterested in what medicine men or priests had to say of death, the hereafter, or the soul. His attitude seemed to be that it was waste of energy to devote thought to such matters, and that one man knew no more of such matters than another. He never entered into theological disputes, I noticed, but he had his own very decided ideas. I asked this old savage philosopher what he thought of Mohammed. He shrugged: "Good for women—maybe!" Before we started back to Nairobi, I gave Tomassie a good pair of shoes, after helping him get a thorn out of his foot, and he appreciated that. Although the most disreputable-looking of all our boys, he was one of the most trustworthy. I used to talk to him sometimes, as best I could. He was entirely frank; he had no wife, no children. He was an even-tempered man, apparently unemotional, yet on one occasion I saw him pull off his coat and stand defiant, ready to fight for his rights, and it was evident that he would resist strenuously. He was no coward.

Kwambe was an intelligent, accommodating boy, and

a thing I particularly liked about him was that he would always give old Tomassie the lighter burden to carry, taking the heavy one himself. I showed my approval by giving him a khaki coat and a pocketknife.

On the trail that morning, we passed some grass huts, where the porters bought and slaughtered a sheep. Since we could not stop to make fire and cook the flesh, they ate it raw, apparently content.

We arrived at our destination in midafternoon. Mrs. Akeley and Raddatz were lying in the shade of a tree awaiting us, and everything was in readiness for the trip to Nairobi the following day.

We started very early. On the way we visited the Evans house, which was attractively situated on a hill. Around it a brave attempt had been made to keep some flowers growing, despite the hot winds of the dry season. Mrs. Evans, senior, a white-haired old lady, told us her son and his wife and children had gone somewhere —to town, maybe. She related how her son had first tried coffeegrowing in Brazil. But labor conditions and politics had decided them to sell out and come to Africa, where they had established themselves as sisal growers. She was a grand old lady—cheerful, wide awake! A native came in for some instructions, and the way that woman could handle Swahili was amazing. It takes a lot of pluck and hard work to learn that language—especially when you are old. Anybody who attempts to acquire a working knowledge of that combination of Bantu, Arabic, Portuguese, English, and others thrown in will share my reverence for this remarkable woman.

We reached Nairobi by nightfall, and found a great deal was to be done there.

BACK TO NAIROBI

As soon as possible after our arrival, I secured a large stretcher, and Raddatz prepared a first-rate canvas for me. On it I started the promised replica of my study for the gorilla group, which I finished in less than two weeks. Mrs. Akeley later presented this picture to the King of the Belgians, as we had planned.

An exhibition of all our studies and sketches had to be prepared, as this also had been promised to the authorities of Nairobi, by Mrs. Akeley, some time before.

This exhibition took place in the Legislative Hall, which is also the headquarters of the Kenya Arts and Crafts Society. It was opened by his Excellency the Acting Governor of Kenya Colony on Tuesday morning, February 15, and was attended by over three hundred and fifty people—a big crowd for Nairobi. I finished the King's picture that Monday morning, hung our eighty-odd studies and sketches in the afternoon, and on Tuesday was on hand all day to receive the visitors and to talk and explain the pictures until evening. Then the studies were taken from their stretchers, packed between oiled papers, and sealed in a tin-lined box for shipping. The expressmen called to take them to the boat, and my part in the first expedition ended.

On Monday, February 21, 1927, I took ship at Mombasa for home by way of Cape Town. I had much to think about on that long journey.

Little had I dreamed, on my arrival in "Brightest Africa," fourteen months before, that when I returned I should leave behind me the man whose artistic vision had supplied the occasion for my visiting the unforgettable scenes I have done my best to describe. My consolation was that on returning to America I might take a further part in realizing that magnificent conception for which Akeley had given his life.

And so it turned out. First, I returned to Africa for additional studies, and later I painted the backgrounds for a number of the habitat groups in the African Hall.

During our association in Africa, Akeley had made his ideas very clear to me, and I could comprehend them perfectly because they agreed with my own. We saw nature and art in much the same way.

Such a spirit as Akeley's does not often appear in this world. He had that rare quality—seldom understood or appreciated because it is so unusual—of complete devotion to art. It was his God.

He was not otherwise religious: not reverential toward conventions, not gentle toward insincerity or compromise, not very particular in the choice of terms with which to express his strong feelings. But he could not be false. His word was to be relied upon. He could be trusted never to betray the cause of art.

Akeley always said that he wanted to die in Africa. He had his wish. In one of the loneliest and loveliest jungles on this earth he lies—lies amid his wild friends, while Nyamlagira stands like a sentinel, its fiery torch a symbol of the flame of genius that lighted his career.

His child—his monument—African Hall remains, with its truth, its beauty, and its deathless significance.

Chapter XXIII

Return to Africa

IN 1928, THE SECOND YEAR after my trip with Carl Akeley, I undertook my second African journey for the Museum of Natural History.

My first intimation that I was to pack up my brushes and return to Africa came when Mr. James L. Clark, of the Museum of Natural History, invited me to supper at his apartment to meet Mr. and Mrs. G. Lister Carlisle, Jr. I found they had decided on a trip to Africa, to collect material for a habitat group of lions that Mr. and Mrs. Carlisle planned to present to the Museum for the African Hall. I was asked to accompany them as painter. In Mr. and Mrs. Carlisle I found two of the most delightful people it has ever been my good fortune to meet. The party was to go to northwestern Tanganyika to the Serengetti Plains where lions were plentiful. We were to secure the specimens and material for background and accessories.

Accompanied this time by my wife, Ethel Traphagen Leigh, I sailed in May, 1928, arrived at Mombasa, and went directly to Nairobi. On our way up I was able to show my wife a lioness from the car window, at daybreak. By that time the rest of the party—Mr. and Mrs. Carlisle, Mr. and Mrs. James L. Clark, and Mr. Raddatz—were already in Tanganyika, with Alfred L. Klein as guide.

In Nairobi, I selected a car for Mrs. Leigh to use in exploring the adjacent country while I went down to do my work in Tanganyika. Raddatz came up with a truck to collect supplies and take me back with him.

Klein's "rock camp" was located three hundred miles south of the railway, only twenty miles from Simpson's Camp site where I had been in 1926, painting studies for the plains group. The country was of much the same character but had less timber. It was prehistoric lake bottom, less than twenty feet above Lake Victoria Nyanza. The most striking features of the landscape—vast level prairies of sun-dried yellow grass—were the immense upstanding granite *kopjes,* which I have already described.

The camp was beautifully situated in a sort of rock horseshoe or amphitheater, open at the southern end only. The position was somewhat elevated. From this south end we had a fine view of the plains stretching away smoothly, interrupted here and there by the rock castles. Cloud masses gathered every afternoon, as the end of the wet season was approaching.

Eight miles away, a low mountain closed in the view. To the southwest rock pinnacles of varying shapes but of uniform character made a saw-tooth horizon.

On the plains, distant herds of animals, dwarfed to the size of crawling insects, appeared and disappeared among the rock castles; sunlit masses against shadows, or dabs of dark paint on light surfaces—wildebeest, kongoni, topi, giraffe, eland, zebra, impala, gazelle, ostrich, bustards; and, among the nearer groups, a Masai herder with his band of sheep.

With field glasses, still smaller creatures could be

The plains of Tanganyika

picked out; jackal, wart hog, guinea fowl. The ubiquitous baboon inhabited the rocks where leopard, lion, and hyenas made their homes except at this season, which was too hot and dry for these fastidious gentry.

Closing in our camp on east and west rose bold cliffs of granite, light silvery pink; their tops strewn with titanic boulders. The dark green of trees contrasted strikingly with these masses, and clothed them with a challenging mystery. To the north, jungle and scattered boulders alternated with grass patches.

Our tents were distributed in a horseshoe curve around three sides of our amphitheater. The dining tent was charmingly situated, beneath trees and amid rocks. In the open center of our horseshoe the trucks were lined up, and a pile of wood stood ready for our evening fire.

Clark's first conception of a lion group envisaged the hour as sunset, just as the animals were preparing to start out hunting.

I therefore began by going out to get a sunset. Each evening I took a truck and drove out to a point about a mile from camp, where I had found a suitable expanse of western sky. During the day I busied myself painting other studies: rocks, plains, trees, or moods of nature.

When a habitat group of such importance is to be done, and especially when it is not definitely fixed as to just what phase of the animals' life will be depicted, many studies should be made. One should know the place so thoroughly that no matter what changes are ultimately decided upon, one will be in a position to do it justice.

The painter who thinks he need make only a given number of studies may find that a brand-new conception will finally prevail, and he will be left with insufficient data. He should secure every study he can. He can never know his subject too well.

Africa is a painter's Paradise—an Eden which has scarcely been touched. Few people dream of the beauty that is there waiting for the right artist. Most of the work that has been done is only a colorless shadow of the reality.

Carlisle had brought a moving-picture camera with him, and he used it constantly. He did not want to kill anything; he merely wanted to take pictures; it delighted him much more to see the creatures alive than dead.

Clark and I consulted and experimented with a field model for the lion group. We abandoned the sunset idea, and tried others. What one sees in the African Hall now is the best of our conceptions. The lions are seen resting in the shade of a tree, near a donga, as is their wont, and beyond them spread the plains. At no great distance herds of animals are grazing peacefully, aware that the hour for hunting has not arrived.

Chapter XXIV

In the Masai Country

To me it is good simply to be alive in Africa. Cities never interest me much: I am not at ease in them. I want to find the places man has not spoiled. In Africa my spirit seems more at home than anywhere I have ever been.

My gun boy on this safari was named Alli. He wore the shorts and coat, without a shirt, that some hunter had cast off, together with a little embroidered skullcap, self-made, and very prevalent in Nairobi. Each cap has a different design, but all are white. Alli wore no puttees because the hunter had not discarded any, but he had automobile-tire sandals.

He didn't seem to know much about firearms—in fact, I think he stood in considerable awe of them. Had any sudden danger arisen while I was at work—if a lion or rhinoceros had approached—I doubt exceedingly whether Alli would have known how to do anything more effective than to cry a warning, and run.

Klein had expected to find water at the rock camp but when he got there he found the supply bad and wholly inadequate. The spring he had reckoned on was at the foot of an upstanding rock—really an immense boulder —from under which, into an eight-foot hole which he had excavated, murky water seeped.

The cook used it for washing pots and kettles, but

Raddatz had to haul our drinking water fifty miles from another of Klein's camps.

One morning I was painting a study of a tree—one of those strange twisted things that one sees only in Africa. It stood beside the path leading to the muddy spring. One of the cook's boys came by, going for water; he soon came back, but his buckets were empty.

"*Hapana maji kwanine?*" (Why have you no water?) asked Alli.

"*Siwesi kwani nyoka!*" (I could not get any because of a snake!)

I sprang to my feet and hurried to the spring, followed by Alli.

Some eighteen inches of the looped body of a large black mamba was visible, protruding from under the rock just above the water. It must have been six feet long or more. The mamba is the most dreaded of all African snakes because of its alertness and pugnaciousness, and because it attacks without provocation or warning. The reptiles reach a length of fourteen or fifteen feet. There are three kinds—black, brown, and green, and all are deadly. They belong to the cobra family. The black mamba inhabits rocks; the olive-brown variety prefers bushes, while the green mamba lives in trees.

"*Mbio! Nilitte bunduki yongu!*" (Run, fetch me my rifle!) I said.

Alli sprinted to my tent, but before he could get back the beast moved out of sight. If we had owned a trained mongoose he might have hunted out the pest. As it was, there seemed nothing to be done. The spring promptly became taboo.

I went back to painting my crooked tree.

Often during late afternoon, while painting my sunset studies, I would see an old hyena come up out of his wart-hog hole, his shaggy coat all awry, his miserable tail depressed, the personification of gloom and dolor. With the usual lugubrious mien he would proceed a hundred feet toward our camp. Then he would halt, and stare at me with his unblinking codfish eyes. He studied me as a scientist studies a protoplasm through a microscope—he analyzed me, and assigned me to the category of meat— desirable but inaccessible. He moved on another hundred feet toward camp and stopped again. He seemed to be reflecting profoundly: On the one hand if he were lucky, he would find a few well-stripped bones in camp; at worst, some bits of discarded dishrag, a shoe, po-tato peels, a forgotten strap, some eggshells or coffee grounds. On the other hand, here was an abundance of succulent, toothsome meat, close at hand—but! He moved on another hundred feet toward camp, and paused. He apparently was reflecting that he must be on the job ahead of his scurvy competitors who were hiding in the bushes. I watched that hyena with a certain commiseration, for are we not all hyenas, in a sense?

When my hyena emitted his dismal howl, I realized, as never before, all the anguish and elemental ruthless-ness of his wild cry of hunger. It seemed to reverberate around the world—to be echoed in the raucous howl of the striking mob—the murderous blood lust of the hag-gard thousands that roar for bread!

Quite near the spot where I was painting, three fennec fox lived in a hole in the ground. With their enormous ears, and bright eyes intent upon me, they seemed to reason, cunningly and with subtle finesse: he is big and unwieldy and slow; he is not concerned with us, anyway; he is doing some queer, foolish thing there; but he is curious, most curious!

When I got up and walked toward them they retreated into their hole, but gradually, without panic. They had me correctly sized up. Not until I was very close did the last head sink completely out of sight.

One evening I was so placed on the plains that a long, gentle elevation of the ground intervened between me and the setting sun. The hill formed my skyline. The sun had sunk behind the unobstructed stretch of grass prairie, leaving an unflecked field of clear rose-lemon, when, exactly upon the crest of the eminence, silhouetted against the sky, a long single-file line of giraffe appeared. A superb bull was in the lead, followed by cows, calves, and other bulls almost as magnificent as the first. It was one of the most impressive spectacles I have ever seen.

Sometimes as I worked whole herds of animals came by. Most of them kept a distance of not less than fifty yards, but their curiosity compelled them to come to a stand and study me. Regiment upon regiment would stop and gaze intently, sometimes for as long as twenty minutes—every individual staring—three hundred, five hundred, a thousand pairs of soft, bright eyes fixed on me. Had they charged in a body I would have had no refuge but the truck, and that they could quickly have overturned. But they had no conception of their power, and, besides, they were not pugnacious. The Thomson's gazelle and the Grant's gazelle did not hesitate to come as close as a hundred feet; they, the most delicate and defenseless of all, were the boldest.

261

Giraffes in Tanganyika

IN THE MASAI COUNTRY

These plains are the scene of enormous animal migrations southward. Ndorobo native hunters follow them and shoot the wildebeest (gnu) with poisoned arrows for the sake only of their tails, which are fashionable articles of wear among the Wacomba and other tribes. A brisk commerce goes on continually. This wanton slaughter—analogous to those we make of egret and seal—has gone on for unknown centuries. The hunters, strangely enough, do not shoot their arrows straight at the animals but up into the air, so that some of the arrows in falling will wound and poison a few of the beasts.

The migrations of the herbivores have been estimated to involve ten or more millions of individuals. They have been explained in two ways: the failure of grass—eaten up—in one area, and the lure in another area of new grass following the deliberate burning off of the matured growth by the natives, for the purpose of attracting game.

How do the animals know about the existence and location of this new supply of grass?

How do the arctic birds know when and where to fly in their migration to the south? What impels the lemmings of Scandinavia to migrate to the sea, at irregular periods, and swim out until they all drown?

Interference with these migrations may be followed by serious results in Africa. The migrations of the lemmings destroyed the food crops of the Norsemen and precipitated the conquest of England. And the wiping out of our American bison reduced the Indians on our plains to starvation.

We were in the Masai country. Sometimes a Masai

herder would drift, close to our camp, with a herd of cattle, or goats and sheep; occasionally he had a donkey carrying a couple of water gourds. The herder wore a single cotton sheet, draped over one shoulder, and reaching down to his knees. He carried a spear.

Who are the Masai? Nobody knows; but they are definitely not Negroes. What their origin may be, and how long they have been in Africa, neither they nor anybody else can tell. The furthest back their memories go is said on good authority to be perhaps two hundred years.

Yet they undoubtedly came at some remote period from the north as conquerors. They brought with them the art of smelting ore and fabricating iron weapons. Being a conqueror, the Masai is traditionally accustomed to dominate; he is an aristocrat. He found on these shores a people in the Stone Age, utterly incapable of standing against him, as helpless as sheep. He remained a conqueror. Even now the Masai retain the psychology of the conqueror—the mental attitude of the master: they despise labor. About them there is even a suggestion of knight-errantry still lingering, conspicuous in their exaltation of the fighting man.

In the search to find good water nearer than fifty miles, we discovered a series of Masai wells some five miles from camp. These wells consisted of round pits twenty-five to thirty-five feet deep. They were located near a dry stream bed, and there were many of them, old and new.

These wells date back beyond the dawn of history. There were two new holes—at least their bottoms had been newly deepened and enlarged, and one of these had a good water flow. When I saw it a party of Masai were busy deepening it, and at first they refused to allow us to take out any water. We had to agree to kill some game for them; for despite their thousands of fat cattle, goats, and sheep they preferred game. It saved them from sacrificing any of their wealth and hence any social standing.

The Masai regarded us as guests, who were in their country on sufferance, and therefore owed them something. A dignified old chief came and demanded that we kill some game for his people. Accordingly a truck was loaded with savages—jubilant at the prospect of having a ride in the white man's *"gari"* (wagon) and getting a good supply of game. A number of zebra, topi, and kongoni were knocked over, and the Masai had a grand picnic.

The Masai have other effective ways of procuring game for food. One is by means of a wide-meshed netting made of the fiber of the sansevieria plant. During the season the wives will make a large amount of this netting, which is tremendously strong. It always remains pliable, and from year to year the supply of netting will increase, until, when each man's quota is added, there are miles of it. With this a double fence about six feet high is erected. Out in the plains, the ends of this fence are a mile or more apart, but they converge on an opening only a few feet wide, at the brink of a huge pit, thirty feet deep. The earth taken from the excavation is piled about its edges, and behind these breastworks crowd the Masai warriors with bows, spears, and clubs, ready to thwart any animal's attempt at escape over the embankment. A huge drive is then organized, covering a semicircle of miles. The natives beat drums, wave firebrands, sing, and yell, and a vast number of beasts run terrified into the trap.

The Masai are divided into many tribes who have somewhat different customs about killing game. Among the first cousins of the Masai proper are the Samburu, the Nandis, and the Lumbwas. The last two named live in well-watered grass country where they have enormous herds of cattle, and as it is also a great game country, it fairly swarms with lion. Since cattle form the most precious possessions of these people, and since lion find beef very toothsome, a clan of lion-killers has developed in each of these tribes. These clans are the most efficient native lion-killing agencies in Africa.

Cattle thefts by lion cannot all be avenged, for they go on so steadily that the clans would not be equal to the task. Only when the lion's killings become very flagrant, and include, perhaps, a man—the chief calls upon the clan to go into action. As the lion-killers constitute the flower of the tribal manhood, they cannot be asked to intervene without real reason, but the occasion arises often enough. A ceremony precedes the hunt, in which the aid of the gods and the blessing of the chief are asked.

As soon as this is over the hunt gets under way. Thirty to fifty men form a line. They are naked except for breechclouts, and each man carries a shield of buffalo hide and a casting-spear.

The men in the line separate about twenty feet from each other, and in this formation they wade through the grass. When a lion is started they pursue; the lion in flight does not travel much faster than his pursuers; he is not accustomed to running long distances and cannot do so without becoming winded; for, with all his strength, he is muscle-bound. The hunters can run much farther than the lion; inside half a mile, the animal halts. Before he is rested the hunters are upon him again. Generally, but not always, he will run a second time but not so far. He has very little breathing space until the hunters are upon him once more, and he will very occasionally run a third time, but that is his absolute limit. He then stands to fight it out.

The hunters know from experience exactly what to expect; they close in on the quarry in a circle. The lion threatens in several directions, but the circle narrows; since the lion crouches in the highest and thickest grass available, the hunters hold their spears until he exposes himself. One of the most powerful and experienced hunters coaxes him by venturing closer than any of the rest. He knows precisely how far the lion can leap and remains just beyond this distance. The lion's attention becomes fixed upon him; he awaits an opportunity to leap; the other hunters edge closer, every spear poised. When all is ready, the man who is holding the beast's attention leaps forward, and the lion springs at him. As the beast flies through the air the hunter hurls his spear, and instantly dodges, his shield upraised to receive the lion's charge. A rain of spears flashes in the sun, and the lion is pierced by one or several blades; still he fights. Either he has to wheel because his foe has slipped by, or he reaches him, dashes aside the shield, and lays his attacker prone. But now five or six spears have found their mark. He has no time to maul or mangle—he wheels on his enemies; perhaps he succeeds in gashing one with a claw, but now the spears have made a pincushion of him.

Lion-spearing in Tanganyika

In a last, desperate effort he roars, rolls, and rises in gasping impotence, then falls, bending a spear that has pierced his lungs, and is still. Rarely is a man seriously hurt in these encounters; but sometimes one is killed. This does not deter the others; they hold a brief ceremony over the body of the fallen monarch, and are off after another.

The hunters will kill five or six lion in a day, and the hunt may go on for many days. Sometimes two lion are encountered together; in this case they do not stand together: one will run in one direction, the other in another.

In the part of the country where our rock camp was located, the grass was not luxuriant enough for lion to hide in it; they would be found in or near the dongas, and this kind of hunting would not be practicable. In bushes the spearmen would be at too great a disadvantage; until he can be got out into the open the lion is comparatively safe from the native.

Colonel Patterson tells of discovering what he believed was the den of the man-eating lions of Tsavo. Maybe he was right, but that part of Africa is not dissimilar to this.

Because lesser animals resort to dens for safety, we have been accustomed to assume that lion do the same, overlooking the fact that aside from man, the lion has no enemies. They are lords in their domain and have no occasion to hide; they fear no attack. They refrain from molesting certain animals that are too well armed, such as the elephant, the rhinoceros, and the black buffalo. The oryx also they avoid, because he throws his head down between his front legs, bringing his long rapier horns to a horizontal position, and then charges with lightning speed. Those three-foot spears of his will go through a lion as easily as a fork penetrates a baked potato, and the lion knows it.

But there are many things about lion we still do not know.

Why, for instance, does a lion roar?

Every guide I have talked with had a different explanation. One claimed that when the lion starts out to hunt, the lioness—the more efficient killer—stations herself near a water hole, while the lion betakes himself a mile or so away from the water hole, and roars so as to stampede the animals toward where his mate lies in ambush. This, says another, is absurd, involving as it does the principle of concerted planning. Does the lion roar to celebrate the kill, much as a hen cackles after laying an egg; not because she has laid an egg, but because a blind impulse, rooted in a past too remote for tracing, impels her? Others, again, point out logically that lion roar without having killed anything. Is it then a call, a challenge, like the bellowing of a bull? Does it express anger. Is it a threat? Is it a boast?

Lion are not always hungry. When they are, they can be treacherous, adroit, crafty, relentless, and incredibly bold. When they are well fed, they can be amazingly mild, indolently harmless, sleepily tolerant. Wounded, they can become unbelievably ferocious and desperately courageous. But whatever they do, they are imbued with the cat spirit, and there is not a suggestion of the human in them. Many people will dispute this; yet among all the missionaries who flood Africa I have not yet heard of one who has tried to convert the lions to vegetarianism.

Chapter XXV

Black-maned Lions

NEARLY EVERY DAY Carlisle, Clark, and Klein went out in one or more cars to look along the dongas for lions. We needed one big black-maned lion, two or three lionesses, and a couple of cubs. As soon as we reached Africa Klein told us we were too late in the season for cubs, as they were nearly full grown by July.

A large black-maned lion is not easy to find. Indeed, thorn bushes and frequent fights make large-maned lions a rarity; in the wild state they are never as fine as in a zoo or a circus.

Clark, being well aware of this feared he might not get a really fine specimen for our group. This anxiety grew as the days slipped by and no adequate king of beasts presented himself. Thus it was that every day the three Nimrods doggedly persevered, and at night around the campfire discussed the lions they had seen, the places they had visited or hoped to visit next, the chances of success, and the reasons for the scarcity of black-maned monarchs. Clark became convinced he must miss no chance of taking a good male lion, even though the beast did not measure up absolutely to every specification; he could not afford to be too particular.

As a consequence of this nervousness they came back one evening bringing a fine large lion but with little mane, and that not black. We all agreed it was a very

271

Black-maned lion

nice lion—not as majestic as lions could be, but just the same an all-right beast.

But the very next day they sighted a regular whale of a brute, with a really decent black mane—they brought him back. Well, whalelike as he appeared in the field, he wasn't so big, in reality, as the one of the day before; and although he had a better mane, it was not a really good one.

The next day, after a hot all-day drive, just as they were heading home at sundown, they saw a regular sockdolager of an old black-maned granddaddy. He was out of range and making off, but they planned to try for him the following day.

Needles in haystacks are not as hard to find as old black-maned sockdolagers, especially when you are desperately anxious to find them. Nevertheless, after several days of disappointments, they sighted a group of lion which included one black-maned male. All the hunters took long and critical looks at him through binoculars; was he the sockdolager or was he not? Regretfully they concluded he was not, yet he was a splendid specimen; not as black as the lost one, but bigger and blacker than either of those we had. Beyond doubt they would not be justified in passing this one up, so they brought him back. He was the best, but the very next day they happened on one so incomparably better than those we had that they brought him along, too. Well, now we had four lion, one a first-rate one for the central figure of our group, and everybody was happy. Of course, our African Hall would not have the grandest lion ever seen, no, no—but it was one that no museum need be ashamed of.

That night we all sat around the big fire, each with a whisky and soda; a new spirit of well-being was in the air. We discussed the situation from all angles; lions must still be hunted for moving pictures; Carlisle must get an outstanding reel; that was settled, but no more shooting would be necessary. The moon was glorious; as we celebrated a hyena let out a mournful howl so near that it startled everybody into laughter.

One day Clark and Carlisle came upon a group of twelve lion dozing in the shade of a tree, in an ideal photographic pose. So the hunters drove off half a mile, shot an old zebra, tied a rope around its neck, attached the rope to the rear end of the truck, and drove, with the dead animal behind them, back to where the lions lay. They hauled the zebra past the lion, making a complete circle. When they repeated the maneuver still nearer to the lion, they began to show interest on the second trip. The third time around they all exhibited excitement; some started toward the zebra, but halted; finally the bait was dragged so close to them that they came in a body. The rope was cut, and the car moved on.

The lion fell upon the carcass, and when they were thoroughly engrossed, the truck was slowly backed up toward them. Every time a lion raised its head, the truck would stop. Little spasms of suspicion kept disturbing the lions, but only one or two at a time would look up. They could not afford more than a slight, hasty snarl for fear the others would get too much meat. Thus the truck backed up to within twenty-five feet of the felines while Carlisle turned the handle of his camera. The click-clack of the machine soon ceased to attract any attention, and the result was one of the best lion reels ever made in Africa.

A day or so after this episode Clark decided the time had come to secure female lion for the group. Accordingly, three lionesses were brought in on three succeeding days, thus allowing ample time for skinning and curing. But on the third day they found that a superb black-maned mammoth was with the lioness. He was simply too good to be left behind, so he was brought along, to make our fifth and finest male. He is a real beauty.

We considered now that we had all we had come for—eight magnificent brutes. If we could not use so many, the Museum could always sell the specimens to other museums.

After this Clark therefore busied himself doing color studies of plants while Raddatz made plaster casts of the same ones, and Carlisle took numerous pictures of the camp.

This work done, Carlisle, Clark, Klein, and Raddatz went off on a jaunt to the south, beyond the low mountain that shut off our view in that direction. It was on this trip that they went into the country of the Mwana-ya-mwezis, and found the people who had never seen or heard of white men before. These were the survivors of a village which had been raided by the Masai: a miserable, cowed, and wretched aggregation, half-starved in a land that teemed with game and produced abundant crops.

After the museum work was done, I drove seven miles daily, out to a water hole to make a picture for Mrs. Carlisle. This pool lay in the bed of a watercourse which

Lions being baited for picture-taking purposes

in the wet season was a torrential river, but had now
shrunk to only a sparse chain of small bodies of water,
some of them heavily charged with soda, alkali, salt, or
alum. Some were shallow, transparent, several feet deep,
and stained deep brown or black, but they contained
fairly sweet water; others were covered with scum,
lettuce-green algae, or the leaves and flowers of lotus.
These water holes even the thirstiest animals appeared to
shun; the cleaner ones they visited regularly. In many
places along the bed of the stream long strips of water
grass grew four or five feet high, dark green, coarse, and
tough. Enough water seeped through to account for
acres of grass.

There is a rock barrier at the northern extremity of
Lake Victoria Nyanza, over which rushes an immense
volume of water—Ripon Falls: it is here the Nile begins.
A bronze tablet says it was discovered in 1862 by J. H.
Speke. Yet only this narrow strip of hard rock stands
between present conditions and others totally different
—possibly vastly less advantageous for man. For millions of years the water has been eating away implacably
at this rock rib. Ages past, when the barrier was twenty
or thirty feet higher than it is now, the lake was much
deeper, and many times more extensive. The grassy
plains where I sat painting were all lake bottom then—
the home of crocodiles and hippopotamus; the rock *kopjes* which dot them now were islands, where pelicans,
flamingos, and fish eagles perched.

Yet many surprises still remain. During the rainy season the level of Lake Victoria Nyanza rises, and the
water backs up along these stream beds for many miles.
Large fish from the lake, lured by the rich supply of

food in the streams, penetrate miles and miles inland. And, like all successful adventurers into new realms, they tend to become fat and lazy, to relax, to take things easy. They have come into possession of natural resources, are the undisputed lords of certain deep pools. Their present comfort induces them to forget that there ever was a lake; it has become only a disagreeable memory, a past full of fierce competition and bitter struggle, a nightmare that may now be dismissed. Swarms of nutritious flies and moths crowd the pool every evening; fat worms and succulent slugs multiply in prodigal profusion. Why worry?

But one day a truck full of black boys stops alongside the pool, and a miniature French Revolution ensues. Husky plebeians leap into the pond and catch the effete gourmands with their bare, black hands! The unwieldy sluggards hide in the darkest holes under the banks, but the vulgar mob hauls them out, and bears them, with howls of bestial glee, triumphantly to camp.

After one such catch our boys brought back many fish three feet long or more, weighing forty or fifty pounds each.

We didn't eat any; we thought the flesh was probably coarse or rank. As a matter of fact, it may have been delicious—we never discovered, for the boys gobbled up every morsel in record time.

The pool I had selected for Mrs. Carlisle's picture was one of the more shallow ones, with fairly transparent water. It was fringed about on two sides with water grass, and had a few rocks in the foreground. In the rear a clump of palms stood above the red-brown grass knolls. It made a pleasant composition—it breathed the

typical loneliness of the African solitudes. It was one of
the best things I painted in Africa.

At the camp we heard lions roaring almost every
night, as we sat around the dancing flames of our fire.
There was something droll in our luxuriating there, in
well fed security, and listening to those other kings of
beasts, also well fed and secure—except from us.

It's a pleasant feeling to be on the top of the heap,
lording it—wallowing in conscious ascendancy over all
the beasts of the earth—all save a few assorted germs
and microbes! As we clinked glasses and cracked jokes,
there seemed to be something comic in the vociferations
of those monarchs whose hides we were after.

It was quite lawful for us to drink whisky—we lords
of the universe—but not for the black boys who served
it to us. For we possessed self-control—hum! We are
superior—I'm not laughing—we really are, you know—
no doubt about it!

An elderly Masai came in to camp to report that he
had lost two cows the night before; two lions had come to
his corral—would we help him—that is, avenge his loss?
Clark, Raddatz, Klein, and I hopped into a truck, took
the Masai in, and drove to his boma.

On the way the man told us one cow had been carried
off, while one was left dying in the corral. Arrived, we
found the typical thorn-bush boma, circular in form, six
to seven feet high, and as good as any the Masai make.
It was situated in a niche among rocks.

The wives of the native were trying vainly to do something for the wounded cow, who lay on her side in the
corral. The only marks on her body were three claw

279

holes on her forehead, but the brain matter was oozing out. She had received one blow, and was beyond help.

The man explained, pointing out the spot whence he had witnessed the whole moonlit tragedy. Two lions had come to the outside of the fence. He had stood with his herder's spear ready, between the cattle huddling in the rock-end of the boma, and the thorn fence. As one lion leaped the fence, the herder had attempted to interfere, but the lion was in an ugly mood. It had boldly passed him by and struck two cows in quick succession. One was stunned, the other killed outright. In an instant the feline picked up the dead cow, and carrying her, vaulted the fence!

We asked for the exact spot; he showed it. There was not the slightest breakage or crushed appearance; that part of the fence was even with the rest—a good six and a half feet in height. The man's statement was incredible. The cow, he said, was quite as big as the wounded one—a well-grown two-year-old Indian cow. Yet the women backed up every statement he made; they, too, had witnessed the killing.

That any animal half the size of the cow could have performed such a gigantic feat of strength as to clear the fence, freighted with such a load—it simply seemed impossible! If I had known enough Swahili to ask the questions I would like to have asked, I would have ascertained just how the lion seized the cow—on what part of her body he took his grip. His technique remains a baffling mystery to me today. He must have seized her somewhere near the middle so as to balance the weight; but her bulk at the middle of her body would seem too great for the span of the lion's jaws.

We hunted outside the fence for signs of blood, for
tracks in the dust, for any indication of dragging; there
was not a sign. Not even a dangling hoof had left a
groove in the sand! The Masai showed us the route the
lions had taken; he pointed to where he said we would
find them, a mile away.

We drove to a donga, and crawled along its edge, Raddatz at the wheel. As we drew near the point the Masai
had pointed to there were the two marauders. One, the
smaller of the two males, was moving about near the edge
of the donga; he had probably been down for a drink.
On the crest of a gentle knoll, silhouetted against the
sky, was the other, keeping guard over the dead cow,
which lay a few feet from him. A half circle of vultures
stood in a dense regiment around the carcass, ready to
pounce upon it the instant the lion relaxed his vigilance.

The lion at the donga's edge was studying us, trying
to make out what manner of animal we were; the one
keeping guard turned a casual glance toward us, and
then resumed his watching of the vultures.

Clark and Klein studied the lion on the hill through
their field glasses; he was young, but very big. Clark
wanted him. It was too long a shot, so Raddatz turned
the car, and started slowly up the incline.

Instantly the smaller lion began to follow, rapidly
sidling in toward us. When he was within a hundred
feet, Raddatz halted and three rifles were brought to
bear on his highness. He was at once aware that the unwieldy interloper was not agreeable to too much familiarity, and he hastily put greater distance between himself and us. We started on, and reached a point about a
hundred yards distant from the sentry on the hill. He

Lion guarding kill. Tanganyika

did not deign to turn his head a second time. Clark stepped out of the car and took a slow steady aim at the back of the lion's head. A fight among the vultures held the cat's attention, and he remained perfectly still, his face turned away from us.

At the crack of the rifle the lion dropped; he rose half way, and then slumped down and lay still. The vultures rose amid a cloud of dust.

We approached the lion cautiously, yet it did not take long to realize that he was stone dead. The cow was as large as the one left wounded; we looked again, but in vain, for any indication that the carcass had been dragged.

We did not kill the second lion. After all, lions have their rights as well as the rest of us; we couldn't use this one.

The Masai was delighted that we had destroyed one lion, but could not comprehend why we had not killed both.

This feline forms the second in importance in the Lion Group as it may be seen in the African Hall today.

Preparations were now begun for the return to Nairobi.

Chapter XXVI

The Greater Koodoo

CLARK, KLEIN, RADDATZ, and I next journeyed down to Mt. Kilimanjaro, in Tanganyika, to secure new material for the greater koodoo group. Mr. and Mrs. Carlisle invited my wife, meanwhile, to accompany them —they in their car, she in hers—on a drive to and around Mt. Kenya. Ethel had a Uganda boy, Hassin, who accompanied her everywhere, and kept her car in first-rate order.

In 1926 Akeley and Daniel E. Pomeroy had agreed that the latter should go down to Tanganyika and procure the koodoo specimens for the group he was to donate, with Lake Hannington as the background. The intention was to include, with the animal exhibits in the African Hall, as many landmarks of Africa as possible. Later, upon reconsideration of our project, it was realized that the koodoo supplied the best opportunity of including Mt. Kilimanjaro, which was a far more important landmark than Lake Hannington. The plans were therefore changed, and the material gathered at the lake was reserved for use in another group—possibly the black rhinoceros, who would fit into that setting quite as appropriately as the koodoo. Another argument, although it carried less force, was that koodoo still existed in the vicinity of the mountain but had vanished from the lake.

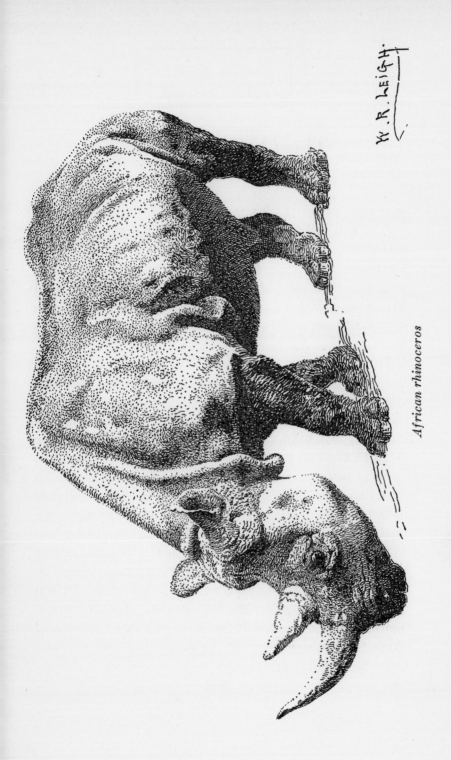

African rhinoceros

W. R. LEIGH.

Our road took us southeast, through a Kenya game reserve. We traveled in three machines, Clark, Klein, and Raddatz driving.

Kilimanjaro at its base is only some three thousand feet above the sea, or three thousand feet lower than Nairobi. The journey consumed three days each way, but the road was good, the scenery fine. The country was full of giraffe, impala, zebra, and other herbivorous game, which we saw constantly. Elephant, buffalo, and rhinoceros also abounded, but we did not see any.

It was ideal rhino country—one might appear anywhere, under any bush. A rhino lying down may very easily be mistaken for a rock, but hard as we looked we did not discover a single one. During the afternoon of the third day I was riding with Clark, and chancing to glance upward through the boughs of trees, was amazed to glimpse, floating in the purple zenith, a mass of exquisite tea-rose pink. I could scarcely believe my eyes. I was looking at the sunlit snows on the dome of Kilimanjaro, "the demon-infested mountain." This was the dome I had seen from Lukenia. This was the mountain of eternal snow that early missionaries had reported, only to be laughed at by the scientists. This was the summit lifted 19,718 feet into the air—the king of all the African mountains.

Airplane photographs have been taken of this dome, which has a huge roughly circular crater 650 feet deep and 6,500 feet across. The mountain has been in eruption, probably, within the last thousand years. This is conjectured from the clear contours of the crater, and from the name, Demon Mountain, which doubtless represents a tradition, or perhaps a memory, of the time when it was active. A thousand years is a short time in the life of a volcano; it may become active again. But we did not get a real opportunity to see Kilimanjaro until we reached Moshi (Smoke), where we halted to pay our respects to the British representatives.

By this time we had traveled down to the southeast side of the peak, and as we approached the end of our journey, I was in an agony of suspense to find out from what angle I would get my view of the mountain. For, obviously, my study was the chief object of the trip down here, and the peak of Kilimanjaro had already been decided upon as the dominant feature of our background. I had already pictured in my mind the view I wanted under these circumstances—the view which would be right for my composition. The picture was to represent sunset, with the sun itself already obscured behind hills while its last light would illuminate the snow fields. The whole lower part of the picture must be in shadow—for that is the hour at which the koodoo become active—and the rosy zone of sunlit snow would float, as it were, in a field of pearl and amber. All this I had predetermined. But now that we were here, would I be fortunate enough to reach a vantage point which would correspond to this prevision?

We left Moshi about five o'clock and traveled fifteen miles across grass plains to a river lined with trees; we made camp in the edge of the jungle.

The country was new to us all, even to Klein, and we had to do a little exploring. Meanwhile Kilimanjaro had vanished in a blank gray haze. If we had told a new arrival in the country that only fifteen or twenty miles away stood the greatest peak in Africa, he would have laughed, and suggested that we were drunk or dreaming.

The place we had selected for our camp was pleasant enough. We were about a hundred yards from the river, which was hidden by jungle. The trees were large, and under them grew a dense mass of bush and giant weeds, fifteen feet high. The tops of the trees were immense, shaggy, black-green masses; vines connected them, and monkeys and parrots infested them.

The next day, being in need of fresh food, we explored some of the country on our side of the river, and secured a lot of quail.

On the third day, however, we broke camp and moved. The road led us to a rather primitive ferry, where a cable had been rigged up and a boat operated by the use of pulleys running on the cable. Three natives lived in grass huts beside the road, and attended to the ferrying.

Having crossed the stream, we followed a road that led away from the river at right angles, through a dense jungle about two hundred feet wide. The jungle ended suddenly, and before us lay plains, covered with grass that was breast-high and half ripened. We left the road, turned to the right, into the grass, and plowed through the waving ocean of feathery seed fronds, parallel to the jungle. Proceeding thus a bare two hundred yards, we turned into the jungle again and stopped under huge trees, whose drooping boughs barely allowed us to pass beneath. Under these mammoth trees the ground was bare, level, soft, and dry. We were once more by the riverside and almost opposite a banana grove and a deserted native village.

A more ideal camp site was never imagined. The shade

was dense and cool, and as soon as the boys had raked away the dead leaves and fallen sticks, the place was clean and open, with only the columnal tree trunks supporting the high green roof.

Our tents were set up facing the river, and between them and the stream tables were arranged, and chairs placed. The view of the water was unobstructed save by the great boles. The shade was perpetual; the sun never got through our canopy of leaves. There were no mosquitoes, no flies, no ants, no pests of any kind. The earth was soft as a carpet under the feet; the torrent made a pleasant rippling sound. There was no indication that the stream ever overflowed its banks; no driftwood was lodged among the trees; no washing of the soil was visible.

Even before we had our tents up we became aware that the tops of the trees above us constituted a regular highway, traveled all day in both directions by whole troops of monkeys. At first we thought the movement and the rushing sounds were made by the wind, but we soon realized that the wind must be singularly localized; across the river the banana leaves did not move. A few chatterings, a glance upward, and we knew. The simians paid no heed to us; they traveled back and forth with a businesslike steadiness; big old men, mothers with babies, young striplings.

The next day, after a delightful rest, I took a truck, and driving back to the road, followed it out across the grass plains. The grass became shorter as I reached the farther side of the open spaces, and I encountered thornbushes. I was nearing the ridges, which were covered with low, stunted trees and bush, in varying shades of purple-brown, burnt yellow, lavender-green, gray, buff, and red. Between them the yellow grass and black rock-croppings were conspicuous. Finally, the way turned directly toward the ridges, and I found I was driving through a pass.

I paused here, and mounted the roof of the machine. With a feeling of immense surprise and satisfaction I beheld Kilimanjaro looming grandly above the strata of mists. When I started I had been under this blanket of obscuring vapor. As if suspended—floating in space— the superb peak made a thrilling spectacle. I drove a mile farther, and turned off the road. Here I got out to ascend a little rocky eminence.

It was the spot I had been hoping to find! Between me and the mountain peak rose spurs of hill which would be just right to hide the setting sun. I could see that when the day was drawing to a close the snow fields would have just the right amount of illumination for my picture. Luck had been with me. I had picked the exact spot from which to work. I was raised above the plains high enough to give me a fine view of them, and still was low enough for the brown hills surrounding me to afford excellent lines and sufficient bulk to balance the mountain. The foreground was ideal for placing the animals, and in my imagination I could see the whole picture finished. So, easy in mind, I returned to the car and retraced the seven or eight miles I had come.

Immediately after lunch, I piled all my paraphernalia into the truck and drove back to my chosen spot. I was in high spirits; there was nothing more to worry about. I got the whole study ready to mass in as soon as the right hour arrived, when the sun would sink behind the hill before me.

Everything developed just as I knew it must. The exquisite island of magical pink, swimming in an opalescent ocean of delicate tones, appeared at the appropriate hour, as if intentionally arranged just to suit me. Below it everything was in shadow—the luminous crepuscule of a world which had just turned from the sun but was still bathed in light reflected from the sky.

I worked madly for the thirty minutes during which the effect lasted, and when twilight finally closed in, I knew that I had reproduced very exactly on canvas the large impression of which I had been dreaming.

With a feeling of well-being and comfort, I made my way through the thorns back to the car, Alli taking everything but the canvas, which I carried myself. I placed it in a position that would preclude any possibility of smearing, or of dust settling on the wet paint, and tied it securely in its position; then I covered it with a tarpaulin and fastened that on.

All this care is indispensable to procure reliable studies in difficult country. Unless a wet canvas is protected, dust, seed pods, straws, insects, will be blown against it. If it is carried any distance, switches will scrape it, and grasshoppers and ants will crawl over it, tracking green paint from the painted trees all over the sky. Bees and moths will paste their bodies against it in full career, and then wallow and slop about trying to extricate themselves. Mosquitoes will leave their wings and legs plastered against the most delicate and conspicuous parts.

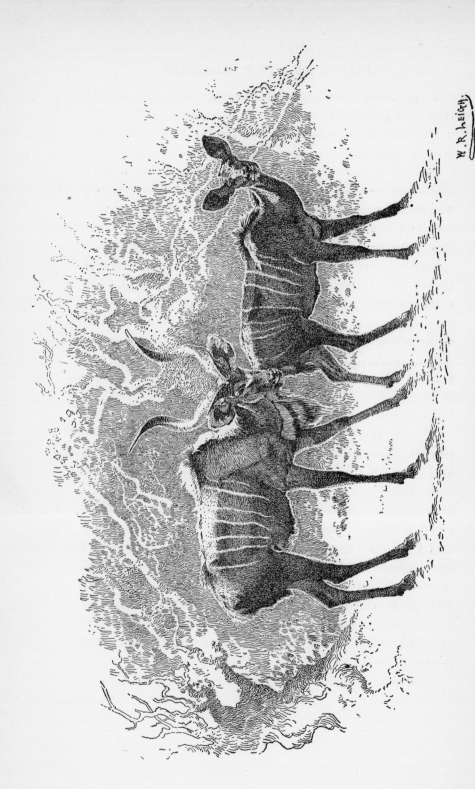

The greater koodoo

THE GREATER KOODOO

Every afternoon from then on I sat atop my hill, with Alli dozing behind me.

One afternoon, while I was absorbed in my work, and Alli sat looking on in his half-asleep fashion, I became conscious of movement down the hill, in the little glen that separated me from the next eminence. The distance was something over a hundred yards, the time near sunset. As I looked, I saw several greater koodoo bull cows step into an open gap, and stand motionless, heads turned to stare at me. They saw me at the same moment that I saw them; each of us kept perfectly still. The wind was in my favor; the koodoos' large black eyes, big ears, and sensitive nostrils were all focused, trying to make out what I was. They stood a good five minutes. Then, concluding I was harmless, they went on their way toward the plains and the river, proceeding with long deliberate strides, smooth and rhythmical, the very embodiment of grace.

The big thrill came the day I discovered a band of elephants down on the flats. It was about half-past three, and I had not been long on my hill. As I glanced out over the wide expanse of bush country between the hills and the strip of grass which followed the course of the river, a flicker caught my eye. I looked more carefully, and I guessed that what I saw was the moving body of an elephant. My doubt was removed when the animal got to an open place and the white tusks became plainly visible. I seized my binoculars, and found that, only about a mile away, the bushes were alive with elephants! As nearly as I could count, there were over a hundred beasts in the herd.

It was amazing to observe their leisurely gait, their

293

rather ponderous movements, which, however, never had to be repeated. A lithe trunk would rise deliberately and grasp a heavy limb on a tree; the limb would come off as though it were made of cheese. With the utmost composure, the beast would then strip the leaves from the bough. Another elephant would walk leisurely up to a tree as big around as a man's body and place his head against it. The tree would tilt farther and farther and finally fall to the ground. Then the pachyderm, perhaps with the help of a calf, would methodically cull foliage, while its huge ears flopped back and forth, and its trunk performed prodigies of slow efficiency. Another monster would seem to be feeling about with its trunk over a patch of sand; then it would lift its great tube in the air, and blow a heavy shower of dust all over its back. Apparently insect pests disturbed even these horny-hided titans.

I saw one beast rip off a limb and use it as a fan with which to drive away flying insects. Another got down on his knees and seemed to be digging with his tusks, or to be whetting them against the sod. There was an absence of haste, a majestic leisureliness, common to everything they did; hurry, uneasiness, impatience, had no place in their scheme of things.

For more than an hour I forgot all about my painting, as I contemplated that extraordinary sight with my glasses glued to my face. Watching these brutes, I realized what scale—size—mass, does. We have all noticed the jerky, lightninglike movements of a mouse, the nimble agility of a squirrel or a monkey. Our own movements seem slow and ponderous by comparison. But the measured deliberation of these Gargantuans bears the

same relationship to our motions as ours bear to the
jerky motions of the mouse. And just as a man can outrun a mouse, so an elephant can easily outrun a man.

To escape an elephant a man must dodge and hide.
The elephant's sight does not seem to be very keen, and
his brain does not work as quickly as a man's. In consequence, if a man slips out of sight behind some object,
the elephant is left in doubt as to whether or not he
really saw something. If a man hugs a tree and remains
motionless, a charging elephant is almost certain to pass
him by without noticing him.

A native I met, who spoke comparatively good English, told me that when he was a young man he had been
gunbearer to a celebrated English ivory poacher whom
he had often accompanied into the most perilous cover
—the bamboo. On nearing the herd, he said, the poacher
would take his best rifle, look it over, then motion his boy
to hide himself. From the high branches of a tree, or on
lofty rocks, paralyzed with fear and astonishment, he
had watched the ivory thief's performances. The hunter
would walk into the midst of the herd. An elephant
would see him, and charge. The man would dodge behind
a bush, a tree, a rock, and glide swiftly, in sudden spurts,
from cover to cover. He might be charged six or eight
times, only to vanish. While the confused beasts cogi-
tated, he crept dauntlessly on, traversing the whole herd
and locating the best tuskers. He slipped like an eel, slid
like a snake. Once three elephants started for him from
three different sides. He was closely pressed, but escaped
by dodging under the belly of a fourth monster. On this
occasion, the native said, the buccaneer killed two enormous bulls, and never got a scratch. The native said he

had been a gunbearer all his active life—he was fifty-five —but that this had been his most hair-raising experience.

As I sat on my rocky hill and watched those lords of the earth, I thought of the vast herds of their near cousins which roamed North America in prehistoric times. They were bigger even than these, their mighty tusks grew up in giant curves that would seem to have rendered them quite useless. To this day these tusks—fossil ivory—are shipped from Alaska in large quantities. The next day Clark and Klein got mixed up with my herd of elephants. They wanted to get near enough to make some photographs but, before they realized it, found themselves right in among the beasts. An elephant saw Clark, who quickly jumped behind a bush and beat a hasty retreat. I decided I would include this herd of elephants in my picture. They may be seen in the background of the koodoo group in African Hall.

The fantasies of poets or painters become pale and arid, when compared with the reality of such a place. No human imagination can suggest its strange allure, its inexpressible loveliness. The painter, or any artist in any medium, finds himself bankrupt—totally inadequate. He feels like creeping into a hole. All that saves him is the reflection that, inadequate as he is and his pigments are, no mere man is any better off.

Seated on my stony hill, which is solid, rigid beneath my feet, I know that these are relative terms—nothing is firm or rigid; these very hills forming the foreground of my picture are evidence of the throes and agonies by which mountains are born. Where Kilimanjaro now rises was once a level plain, and where I sit was once the bottom of the sea. This picture I paint—which seems im-

portant to me, into which we will all of us put our sin-
cerest efforts—the best materials extant, with the hope
that it will impart some hint of the reality, and endure,
perhaps, two or three hundred years—this picture is an
ephemeral thing. This soft lump which is I, wielding a
clumsy brush—hungering for the impossible—striving
to tell of the marvels that are before me—this shadow
which has to dodge lest the thorns tear and the stones
bruise it—will fade—fade faster than the poor thing it
puts on canvas.

All but beauty will pass—beauty will never die. No;
not even when the earth and the sun have died will
beauty perish. It will live on in the stars.

And now these rugged, savage hills around me, so
sere, so harsh with rock and snag, stand purple-brown
against the daffodil field of sunset sky.

As in a trance I turn, the finished study in my hand,
and, in the fast-growing shadows, wend my way down
by the devious path imposed by the wait-a-while thorns.
I am leaving my little hill for the last time—I will see
the sublime spectacle of Kilimanjaro at sunset no more.
Alli follows with umbrella and paintbox; he looks at the
finished study stolidly. It is impossible for him to understand why the foolish white man should go to so much
trouble and expense to get anything so useless. He will
tell his friends about it, and they will laugh, but remark
that the fool white man is a good cow to milk—he must
never know what a damned fool the Allis know him to
be.

Now my study is made fast in its place and covered
against the dust. I take my seat behind the steering
wheel, but before I put my foot on the starter I take a

W. R. Leigh

Mt. Kilimanjaro

long look at the mountain. The shadows are creeping, creeping up; the field of rose is changing, growing smaller, dimmer. Night approaches—the stars, the moon. As your light fades, my lovely peak, so will mine; but my record will not change—for a while. It will endure for a little time, that those at home may gaze upon it, and, maybe, sense something of what I have tried to paint and to write.

NOTE ABOUT THE AUTHOR

WILLIAM ROBINSON LEIGH *is one of the foremost living American painters of natural scenery and wild life. Born in 1866 in Berkeley County, West Virginia, he spent much of his boyhood living out-doors, hunting birds and animals, fishing, tramping, farming, and studying and painting nature in all its aspects at all seasons. He then studied art at the Maryland Institute in Baltimore and lived for twelve years in Munich where he continued his studies at the Royal Academy, winning medals for three years in succession and receiving an honorable mention in the Paris Salon of 1892. He has painted and exhibited many landscapes and figure and ani-mal compositions as well as six cycloramas. He ac-companied the Carl Akeley Expedition to Africa in 1926–27 and the Clark-Carlisle Expedition the next year to make sketches for the backgrounds of the African animal-habitat groups in the American Museum of Natural History of New York. From 1932 to 1935 he worked as master painter in the famous African Hall of the museum. He is also the author of numerous articles and short stories on American-Indian and African themes and has writ-ten two books,* Clipt Wings *and* The Western Pony.

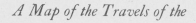

A Map of the Travels of the

AMERICAN MUSEUM EXPEDITION

in which Mr. Leigh was concerned

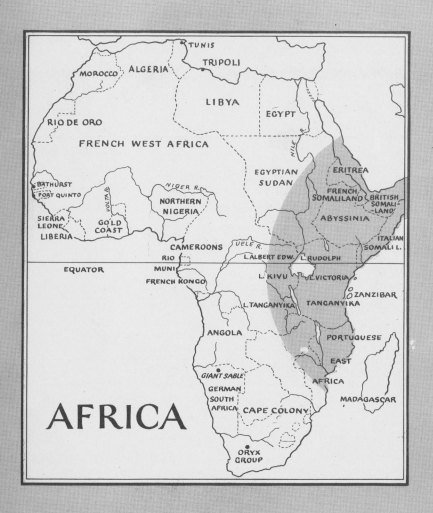

TUNIS
MOROCCO ALGERIA TRIPOLI
RIO DE ORO
LIBYA
EGYPT
FRENCH WEST AFRICA
EGYPTIAN ERITREA
SUDAN
BATHURST FRENCH
PORT QUINTO NIGER R. SOMALILAND BRITISH
NORTHERN SOMALI-
SIERRA VOLTA R. NIGERIA LAND
LEONE GOLD ABYSSINIA
LIBERIA COAST
CAMEROONS UELE R. ITALIAN
RIO SOMALI L.
EQUATOR MUNI L. ALBERT EDW. L. RUDOLPH
FRENCH KONGO L. KIVU L. VICTORIA
ZANZIBAR
L. TANGANYIKA TANGANYIKA
ANGOLA
PORTUGUESE
EAST
GIANT SABLE AFRICA
GERMAN
AFRICA SOUTH MADAGASCAR
AFRICA CAPE COLONY
ORYX
GROUP